FROM THE BEGINNING
❖ 1905-2005

A Century of Excellence
University of Nebraska at Kearney

By Susanne George Bloomfield

Richard D. Schuessler

Eric Melvin Reed

2005 University of Nebraska at Kearney
ISBN 0-9745410-8-7 (soft bound)
ISBN 0-9745410-9-5 (hard bound)

FROM THE BEGINNING, 1905

Before the voters spoke, twenty acres yearned

To be small rooms past which a tail-race ran

With inarticulate speed. To fill a field

In which there was the grace of one green terrace.

The act once passed, its mortar formed a place

To which a hundred students brought their book–

Bent selves, a study-stead for those who'd try

Their minds upon the boards of understanding.

Around whom something more began to form.

Call it an education, that circumstance

Still drawing us out, that thought-faring

That goes on when every page becomes a pulse,

Each chapter one more verse, a turning

To new lives. Until we go by work, by words,

Into the reaches of ourselves, the commencement

Of who we were, and are, our fortune and surprise.

Don Welch

❖ "Old Main"

INTRODUCTION

T he present day always seems to be the most important. Yet, the more one reflects, the more one understands that all of the days and years that have gone before serve to bring the present into focus. As we celebrate the centennial of the University of Nebraska at Kearney, it is important to understand the history of this institution–and that is the inspiration for this book. It is not intended as an in-depth chronicle, nor is it a coffee table piece. Instead, it is an earnest look at the major events that played a role in the development of this university, and it includes profiles of some of the people who contributed to its success.

The University of Nebraska at Kearney was and continues to be a long-term investment in our future by Nebraska's citizens. This campus, established in rural Nebraska, began as an uncertain asset. Today, more than a century later, it is clear that the investment is paying handsome dividends that are visible state and nationwide.

The success of the campus can be measured in many ways: individual achievements, buildings, technology, or simply by the passage of time. However, the true success of the institution is its enduring commitment to students. This publication recounts the progress, the history, and the traditions of the campus, and it reflects the evolving mission of our university. Without the institution's resolve to advance our students' educational opportunities and to attract and retain first-rate faculty and staff, it would have long ago perished. Today the University of Nebraska at Kearney has assumed a greater role in Nebraska and the region. Since the beginning, the need for greater funding has been our continuing legacy. It will no doubt remain as a hurdle in the future. Despite the odds, the University of Nebraska at Kearney has not only survived but has flourished and triumphed. A steadfast commitment to students has transformed a fledgling State Normal School into a bustling university. This is the story of that commitment.

"From the Beginning" is the culmination of a yearlong effort to research and preserve the history of Kearney's campus of higher education. The authors and the students assisting in the research and design of this book are products of the University of Nebraska at Kearney and are themselves representatives of the quality that surrounds the institution. I want to take this opportunity to thank them for their uncommon commitment and, on behalf of the entire university community, to thank them for recording this history.

GO LOPERS,

Chancellor Doug Kristensen

NEBRASKA STATE
NORMAL SCHOOL
AT KEARNEY

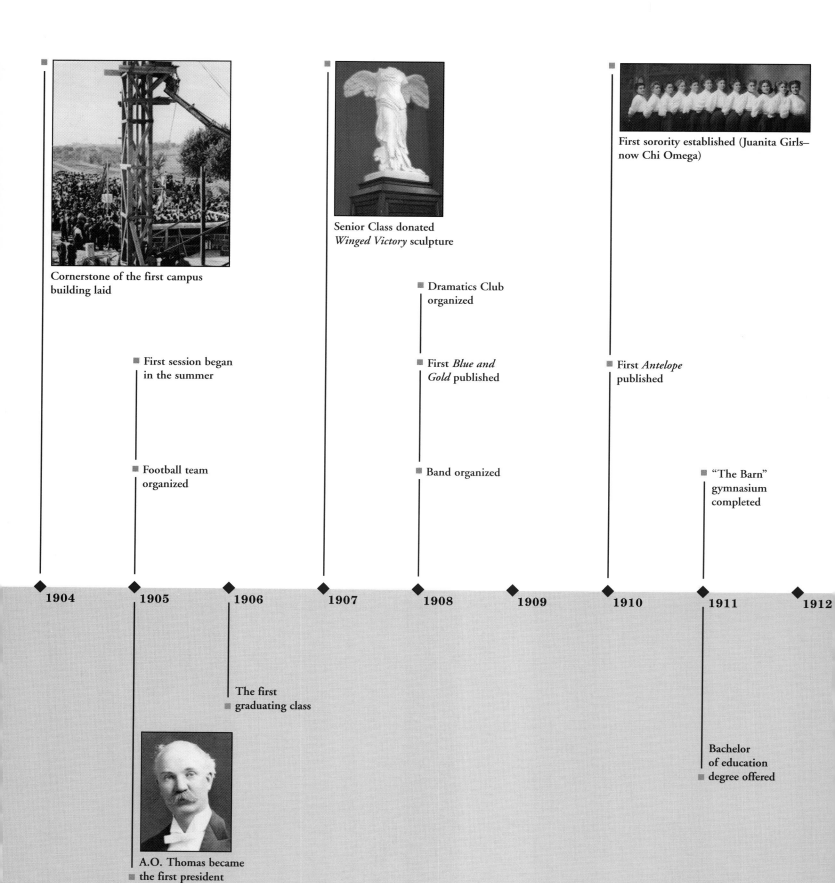

Cornerstone of the first campus
building laid

First sorority established (Juanita Girls—
now Chi Omega)

Senior Class donated
Winged Victory sculpture

Dramatics Club
organized

First session began
in the summer

First *Blue and
Gold* published

First *Antelope*
published

Football team
organized

Band organized

"The Barn"
gymnasium
completed

1904   **1905**   **1906**   **1907**   **1908**   **1909**   **1910**   **1911**   **1912**

The first
graduating class

Bachelor
of education
degree offered

A.O. Thomas became
the first president

NEBRASKA STATE
NORMAL SCHOOL
AT KEARNEY

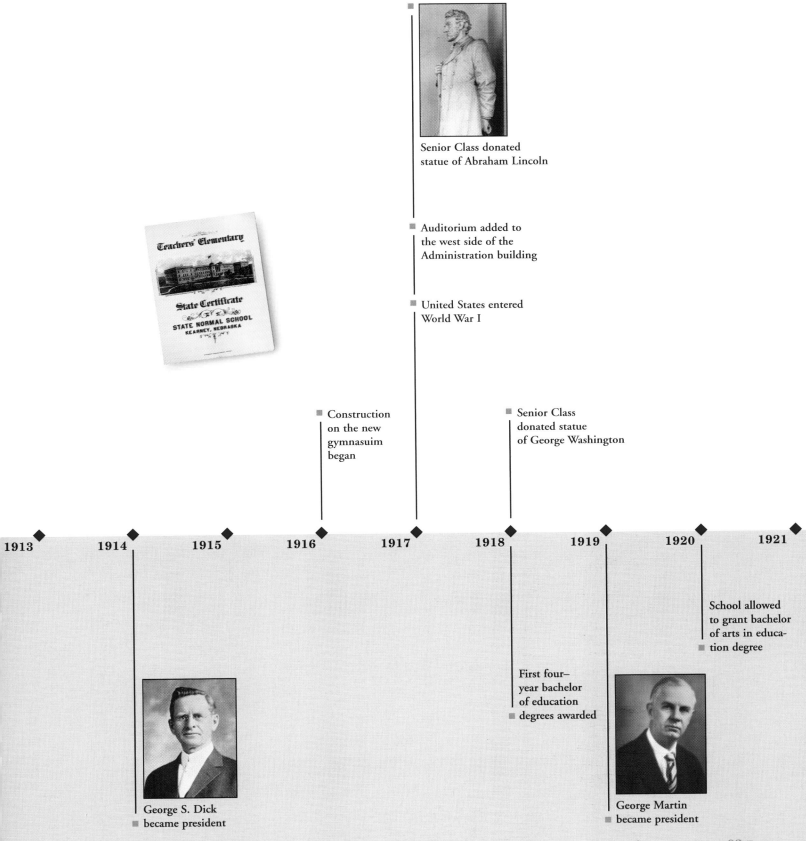

Senior Class donated
statue of Abraham Lincoln

Auditorium added to
the west side of the
Administration building

United States entered
World War I

Construction
on the new
gymnasuim
began

Senior Class
donated statue
of George Washington

1913   1914   1915   1916   1917   1918   1919   1920   1921

School allowed
to grant bachelor
of arts in educa-
tion degree

First four–
year bachelor
of education
degrees awarded

George S. Dick
became president

George Martin
became president

CHAPTER ONE
❖1905-1921

❖ The first session began in the summer of 1905 with Lena Tyler ('07) from Kearney being the first student to enroll on June 19. Later that day 71 others registered for the six–week summer term.

NEBRASKA STATE NORMAL SCHOOL AT KEARNEY

I n 1903 when the Nebraska State Legislature appropriated $50,000 for the establishment of a new normal school in western Nebraska that would be devoted to teacher education, a fiercely competitive, political battle ensued. The communities of Alliance, Ainsworth, Long Pine, Fairfield, Central City, Lexington, Ord, Gothenburg, Broken Bow, St. Paul, Hastings, Holdrege, Aurora, North Platte, and Kearney campaigned to be selected. Each city had to commit at least 20 acres of land, but the economic benefit to the chosen community would be enormous.

❖ BEGINNINGS

As the 20th century opened, emerging towns on the Great Plains competed with each other to attract settlers, railroads, and, especially, new business opportunities. Kearney Junction, incorporated in 1872 at the intersection of the Burlington and Union Pacific Railways, began with a population of 100 people. Renamed Kearney in 1873, the town saw steady growth in its early years, especially after the state designated it as the county seat and the first bridge, a mile long, over the Platte River was built. The town boomed in the 1880s when George Frank constructed 16 miles of canal to furnish electricity to the city, and the population swelled to 12,000, creating a burst of industry, the first electric street cars in Nebraska, the luxurious Midway Hotel, and an opera house. At one point Kearney boosters formed a plan to relocate the nation's capital to the city. However, the nationwide economic collapse of the mid-1890s devastated the city's economy, and in 1901 the population plunged to 5,604. By 1902 the town was slowly beginning to rebuild, and Kearney reported 6,202 residents.

Although bidding for the new Normal School ("normal" comes from the French word meaning "model") would begin in July 1903, by May of that year communities had already started sending delegates to Lincoln to present their proposals. A group of Kearney citizens met on December 16, 1902, to begin enlisting support and organizing several meetings for the spring. On May 5 city hall was standing room only as a crowd of Kearney residents joined together to solicit financial support, arguing that the school would bring 500 more families as well as 1,500 pupils to Kearney within five years, raise real estate values, and give impetus to new businesses.

The State Board of Education spent the month of August 1903 visiting all of the communities that had submitted bids and finally voted on September 1. Kearney presented a bid of $90,000, including Green Terrace Hall valued at $50,000, 23 acres of land worth $10,000, water from Kearney Lake, and

GEORGE ARNOLD

After three years of farming along the Big Horn basin in Wyoming, George Arnold moved to Kearney upon the advice of family friend Dan Morris, president of the State Normal Board. Arnold accepted the position of night watchman at the Normal School in 1915 and was appointed head custodian a year later. He served as chief custodian for 35 years, and upon his retirement in 1951, the college awarded him a lifetime pass to all athletic events.

other considerations. After 111 ballots the board awarded the new school to Kearney, citing its central location, railway accessibility, density of population, and offer of Green Terrace apartments for use as a dormitory. Kearney received four votes, Broken Bow two, and Ord one. When the news broke at 3:15 p.m., the Kearney steam laundry and flour mill whistles started sounding, and soon everything that could make noise in town "let loose."

Ord contested the decision, alleging that Kearney's 20 acres were not uninterrupted, the building was unsuitable, and the whole process was unconstitutional, but the decision stood. Aurora, who had the earliest and strongest community backing, grumbled, "It certainly seems that it is not to be the town that offered the best inducements and clean surroundings, morally, that should be entitled to this school, but the town that could show the least cash, the greater number of saloons, greater numbers of houses of prostitution and ungodly surroundings."

NEW BUILDING ❖ AND FACULTY

In 1904 the State Board of Education selected George A. Berlinghof as architect for the new administration building, which would face the east and be centered on 25th Street with public driveways curving around both ends of the building. Berlinghof designed the 170-by-74-foot building so wings could be added later. Knutzen and Isdell of Kearney won the bid for the concrete stones–finished to represent granite and gray sandstone–at $41,500 for the three-story structure. Two large rooms for manual training and domestic science, four classrooms, and lockers occupied the first floor; a board reception room, two offices, three model schoolrooms, recitation rooms, and restrooms filled the second floor; and the library, chapel, four science laboratories, lecture rooms, and a storeroom were located on the third floor. Contractors paved the halls with marble tile; constructed the windows, doors, and moldings of each room with white oak; wired the building for electric lights; and prepared it for gas and water service.

The Masonic Grand Lodge of Nebraska laid the cornerstone on October 18, 1904, while a large crowd endured a severe thunderstorm with hail. Ceremonies in the opera house provided more comfortable surroundings for speeches by dignitaries such as University of Nebraska Chancellor E. Benjamin Andrews, who commented, "The citizens of the city should see to it that the state makes liberal appropriations for the maintenance and expansion of the institution, so that it may grow and prosper in proportion to the growth and prosperity of the state."

After 102 ballots in May 1905, the Normal School Board designated A. O. Thomas, then superintendent of Kearney Public Schools, as principal. The hiring of faculty members and the assigning of salaries proceeded quickly: M. R. Snodgrass, Wayne, higher mathematics; W. A. Clark, former principal at

Cornerstone ceremony

Laying of sidewalk up to Old Main

JENNIE M. CONRAD ◆

Jennie M. Conrad graduated from the Normal School in 1912. After six years of teaching in secondary schools and a stint at homesteading in Idaho, she returned in 1920 to teach in the social sciences. While on staff at the Normal School, Conrad traveled extensively, visiting 42 countries. She participated in several professional organizations, including the Nebraska State Education Association, where she served as president from 1938–39. After 41$^{1/2}$ years of service, Conrad retired in 1961 as an associate professor after reaching the mandatory retirement age of 70. North Hall was renamed Jennie M. Conrad Hall on October 31, 1963.

Peru Normal School, psychology and pedagogy; Eva J. Case, Red Cloud, preceptress; C. N. Anderson, Tecumseh, American and European history; Wynfred E. Allen, University of Nebraska, biological sciences; Charles W. Philpott, Lincoln High School, physical sciences; George N. Porter, Peru, rhetoric and literature; Gertrude Gardner, Fairbury, Latin language and literature; Alma Hosic, University of Nebraska, German language and literature; Edith L. Robbins, Ord, English grammar and composition; A. J. Mercer, Lincoln High School, geography, agriculture, and manual training; O. W. Neale, North Platte, civics, school law, and arithmetic; H. C. Richmond, South Omaha, music; Marion Smith, Columbus, art; Clarence A. Murch, Kearney, principal of commercial department; Etta Brown, Valentine, superintendent of training department; Mary Crawford, West Point, assistant in English department; Catherine Hicks, Farnam, intermediate critic teacher; Grace Greves, Fremont, primary critic teacher; and Anna V. Jennings, Davenport, librarian. Salary for 1$^{1/2}$ years' service for faculty ranged from $600 to $1,200.

Five faculty committees also formed: Enrollment and Credits; Program and Curriculum; Rules, Regulations, and Discipline; Lectures, Entertainments, and Receptions; and Normal Extension Work. In addition to serving as advisors to the students, the faculty also met in each other's homes for

1905 faculty members

MARY MAJOR CRAWFORD

When the last of the original faculty members retired in 1943, Mary Major Crawford completed her 38th year of teaching. A graduate of the Normal School at Peru (1904) and the University of Nebraska (AB, 1907; MA 1912), she taught in high schools throughout the state and studied at the University of Chicago before being selected as an associate professor of English at the Normal School. Although born in Maine, Crawford insisted that she was a true Nebraskan, having lived in the state since her infancy. An advocate of equal suffrage, Crawford was also an active member of the National Council of Teachers of English and the Nebraska State Teachers' Association.

Students at Kearney Normal

professional development, studying the history of Normal schools the first year.

The first session of the Nebraska State Normal School at Kearney began in the summer of 1905. Lena Tyler ('07) from Kearney was the first student to enroll on June 19, 1905, at 7:20 a.m. Later that day, 71 students registered for the summer term that would last six weeks. Total enrollment for the summer was 120—7 men and 113 women—who attended classes at Longfellow High School and Whittier Elementary.

When the Normal School started its fall term on September 20, 1905, the Administration building was still under construction, so the first week of the session was held at Longfellow High. By the time classes moved to the Administration building on September 25, temporary stairs led from the second to the third floors, window glass had not been installed on most levels, and classrooms migrated from room to room on a daily basis, a task easily accomplished as little furniture

or equipment had yet been delivered. On chilly days two traction steam engines were coupled onto the heating pipes and warmed the building until the heating plant was finished. The noise of hammers and saws echoed throughout the building during lectures, but everyone agreed that carpenters and mechanics should have priority. When chairs and desks finally arrived, three professors helped to hoist the fixtures to the second and third floors and uncrated them.

The estimated expense for the first year of classes was $82,700: $47,500 for salaries; $15,000 for a heating plant; $6,000 for furniture, blackboards, and lab supplies; $11,000 for utilities, sewer, and grounds improvements; and $3,200 for miscellaneous costs. Enrollment of more than 300 students, however, exceeded expectations, and supplies had to be doubled. By the end of November, 396 students had registered for the first session. By the end of the first session with building construction still underway, 430 students had signed up for classes, and 464 students were enrolled for summer 1906. (Enrollment numbers vary depending on the source and compilation methods.) The six-week summer session provided training to area teachers, and like the regular terms, it was free to all residents except for a $5 matriculation fee.

❖ GREEN TERRACE

The remodeled Green Terrace apartments, donated by the city, became a dormitory for women, who were required to live on campus. Three stories high, the brick, red sandstone, and terra cotta structure faced south, about one block from the main Normal School building (where Ludden Hall now stands). Heated by steam, Green Terrace boasted a large reception hall with staircases and immense fireplaces at either end. Furnished with mission-style tables and chairs, carpeted with velvet rugs, and brightened by two large bay windows with porches, the reception room impressed all newcomers. Forty-two sleeping rooms, many with windows that opened onto porches, contained iron bedsteads, dressers with large plate-glass mirrors, washstands with bowls and water pitchers, and desks. Nearly all rooms had a closet, and electric lights added to "the splendor." The third floor rooms, less sumptuous, were also more economical. The dorm rooms were filled by August 31, 1905. Green Terrace also offered six bath and toilet rooms with water available in all parts of the house. However, women enjoyed hot water from the heating plant only during the winter until the first water heater was installed in 1914.

Green Terrace apartments

The basement of the dormitory ran the length of the building and consisted of a dining room capable of seating 400. Fireplaces with large mirrors above them flanked each end of the room. The kitchen, "a marvel of convenience," which stood off the dining room, included a pantry and tanks for dishwashing as well as adjoining rooms for storage and laundry. Perhaps most important to students and faculty alike was the creation in 1908 of a food service, which was a source of concern in the early years of the campus. Mr. and Mrs. John D. Saunders provided high-quality, affordable meals for faculty

Green Terrace dining room

Home of President A.O. Thomas

and students. The Saunders purchased much of the food directly from area farmers or the Normal School farm. The farm supplied milk and butter from the dairy herd, maintained a coop behind the dormitory in order to serve fresh chicken, and raised most of the potatoes. William M. Anderson cooked for the Saunders's food service for 26 years and received $25 a month plus room and board. It is said that he covered each table with a silence cloth and a white linen tablecloth, set all of the tables early, and covered everything with a third cloth. A single light bulb on a drop cord hung over each table. No one took a seat until after the blessing.

President Thomas appointed Eva Case as the first preceptress or housemother of the dormitory. Her job description involved regulating the conduct of the women students, not only in the dormitory but on campus and in the community, as well as overseeing the food service and janitorial staffs. In addition, Case held faculty status and was expected to teach. Upon her death in 1907, Anna Caldwell took her place, followed by Sarah A. Brindley.

In February 1907 President Thomas moved into his new home at 2222 9th Avenue (now the Kearney Alumni Association headquarters), which became the scene of many informal gatherings of faculty, students, and friends of education as well as the site for formal faculty meetings.

PROBLEMS ❖

Financial problems vexed the Normal School from its beginning. By 1907 the Normal School experienced severe overcrowding. Governor George L. Sheldon, however, vetoed appropriations for additions to the original building even though the cost to the state for two years of Normal School education, according to a 1909 study, was $206 per student, compared to $329 in California and $1,250 in Illinois. The state created a new Normal Board to oversee the state's teacher colleges, but its power was questioned and the issue went to court. Meanwhile, the Normal School could not pay its bills, so President Thomas had to personally borrow money (as did Peru's President James W. Crabtree) to meet the payroll. When the court settled the case in 1909, ruling the new Normal Board unconstitutional and reinstating the old board, Thomas was reimbursed for the loan–but not the interest.

In 1913 the Normal Board dismissed President Thomas over the objections of the school and the community for allegedly using the school to further his own interests and seeking employment elsewhere; however, most believed Thomas's outspokenness, independence, and political savvy alienated the board. As a result of Thomas's popularity on campus, the students threatened to walk out of school in protest, for he had earned a reputation for understanding and compassion. In 1908 the yearbook noted, "If teachers are sick, or downcast or overworked President Thomas is the first to note it and at once apply the healing balm; should students become homesick or discouraged, he is never too busy to hear their story, and never lacks for words of comfort, cheer or seasonable advice." Dr. Thomas asked the students not to demonstrate, saying that the school was larger than any one man and that he did not want political dissension to cripple the future of the institution.

The board appointed Dean M. R. Snodgrass as interim president until 1914 when they hired George S. Dick, in part because of his experience in developing a program for the training of rural teachers. At this time the Normal Board also divided the responsibilities of the president, creating the Department of Records under the direction of the registrar, who was to maintain the financial accounts of the institution and the scholastic standings of the students.

World War I caused a drop in enrollment from 451 in the fall of 1915 to 305 by the fall of 1918. However, in the summer of 1918 the school awarded the first four-year bachelor of education degrees to 20 seniors. President Dick also conferred the first rural certificates to 16 teachers. Previously, nearly 45 percent of the students were actually secondary students; with this first graduation, the campus changed from a Normal School to a college. In 1920 the Normal School was given the authority to grant a bachelor of arts in education degree.

In the fall of 1919 President Dick resigned under pressure, with no protest from students, faculty, or community, and accepted a position as educational advisor at the Army Hospital in Denver. Dean George E. Martin became the third Normal School president and would lead the Nebraska State Normal School at Kearney as it evolved into the Nebraska State Teachers College at Kearney.

GEORGE S. DICK

George S. Dick served the Normal School as its second president from 1914 until the end of World War I. During his tenure, the school was transformed from what was essentially a secondary school into a college, issuing its first BEd degrees in 1918. Before joining the Normal School, Dick served as director of teacher training at Iowa State Teachers College. With his experience in developing rural education programs, he created the rural education department, which included four rural training schools. Upon his resignation in January 1919, Dick accepted the position of educational advisor at the Army Hospital in Denver.

Inside the president's office

BESS FURMAN

The first female editor of the Antelope, Bess Furman was also the first female reporter regularly assigned to cover the U.S. House of Representatives. Following her graduation from the Normal School in 1918 and a brief stint as a writer for the Kearney Daily Hub, Furman accepted a position with the Omaha Daily News in 1920. In 1929 she became a member of the Washington D.C. Bureau of the Associated Press and a correspondent for the New York Times, which assigned her to cover First Ladies Lou Henry Hoover and Eleanor Roosevelt. Her first book, *Washington By-Line: The Personal History of a Newspaperwoman* (1949) was a bestseller.

TRADITIONS ❖ Many traditions originated during the early years at Kearney's Normal School, and students and faculty alike looked toward the future. President Thomas hired J. M. Hadkinson, who had designed the building plan for the 1898 Trans-Mississippi International Exposition in Omaha, to create a layout of locations for buildings, driveways, parking lots, trees, and sidewalks for the Normal School grounds "in a scientific and artistic manner." Thomas strictly followed Hadkinson's plan throughout his tenure, especially in the planting of specific trees and shrubs. On May 3, 1908, classes and organizations initiated one of the first campus customs—planting trees on Arbor Day. The school dismissed classes for half a day, and students assembled with shovels to plant trees from the main entrance of the Administration building to 9th Avenue. Next to each tree students buried bottles with the names of the donors inside and named each tree for a faculty member or honored person.

May Day celebration

Another campus tradition that began as early as 1910 celebrated May Day with the winding of the Maypole, which typically began in the morning with the early dismissal of classes. In 1912 faculty and students congregated for a photograph by Lincoln panoramic artist F. W. Beverly. Next, a procession of students in Anna Caldwell's kindergarten department, accompanied by the Normal band, danced to a Maypole, decorated with red and white streamers, where they performed a folk ritual, exhibiting their mastery of the steps they would be teaching their future students. Afterward, students continued the annual "dandelion harvest," picking up litter and digging weeds to beautify the campus grounds. They spent the late afternoon picnicking: the freshman class journeyed to the cotton mill; the sophomore and junior classes feasted at the Wood River; and the faculty, seniors, and commercial students celebrated at the large wooden pavilion on Kearney Lake. This tradition continued until 1937.

Throughout these early years classes and organizations also contributed art to aesthetically enhance the campus, and many still adorn campus buildings. The first public art was a life-size bust of Shakespeare donated in 1905 by the Gonnelle Brothers of Lincoln. The class of 1907 contributed the sculpture *Winged Victory* with the Debating Society providing its oak base. The training class of 1908 presented a bust of Abraham Lincoln while the senior class bestowed *Washington Crossing the Delaware.* Not to be outdone, the training class of 1909 added a picture of *The Oath of Knighthood.* The senior class of 1911 presented the school with the *Parthenon* frieze, and the *Poseidon* frieze was a gift of the class of 1914. The class of 1916 purchased the light posts in the front of the Administration building, the class of 1917 donated a life-size statue of Abraham Lincoln, and the class of 1918 provided a matching statue of George Washington.

❖ CAMPUS EXPANSION

As Kearney's Normal School continued to grow, the legislature recognized the need for expansion, and a flurry of new construction enlarged the campus. In 1910 the school added a 361-by-123-foot north wing, the Shellberger, to the Administration building. Its fireproof floors were constructed of reinforced concrete covered with heavy battleship linoleum made of finely ground cork and white lead. The building was said to be dustproof because it could be cleaned with a damp mop. Italian artisans laid Venetian marble terrazzo in the halls, polishing it to bring out the gray body and red borders. The first floor housed the general library, and Thomas asked faculty to recommend books to fill it. The student matriculation fund supported their purchase. When the library moved into the north wing in 1911, it contained 6,000 books and subscriptions to 101 periodicals, and a reading room with 8 tables and 80 chairs. Anna Jennings, Floy C. Carroll, and Alice Paine directed the library, with Jennings serving from its beginning until 1937. On the second floor, the east end was devoted to art, including pottery, and the west end was designated for music, reading, and elocution. Biological and agricultural sciences and labs occupied the third floor.

In 1912 the school added a south wing, the Aldrich, which duplicated the earlier addition to the north. The first floor accommodated the model schoolrooms and vocational arts; the second housed German, education, penmanship, and mathematics; and the third held physical science.

Construction began on a new gymnasium in 1916, but because of World War I, progress was slow. When it was completed, the structure first housed

Class of 1911

BRUNO O.
HOSTETLER

Bruno O. Hostetler was a leading influence in helping to establish the Normal School in 1903. He graduated from the University of Iowa in 1885 and obtained a law degree from that school in 1887. He then moved to Kearney, where he practiced law and was elected mayor in 1898, 1899, and 1900. In 1903 he ran and won the race for judge of the 12th Judicial District of Nebraska, serving nine terms from 1904 to 1941. In 1980 Hostetler's daughter, Florence Raymond, provided funds for construction of an amphitheater in honor of her father's memory.

the Student Army Training Corps. It contained a swimming pool, a large shower with bathrooms, and faculty offices on the ground floor; a basketball court on the second floor, and other physical education facilities on the third floor. Classrooms also occupied all three floors, and the building offered a large room for social gatherings and a kitchenette.

Interior of new auditorium

As the student body continued to increase, an auditorium in the Administration building became a necessity since the school strongly encouraged students and teachers to attend daily chapel convocations, featuring faculty as well as invited speakers, musical and theatrical programs, and even pep rallies. In 1917 a 110-by-80-foot addition to the west side of the Administration building was completed. Although construction lagged because of the difficulty in obtaining steel and other materials during wartime, when finished, it seated 1,500 people. Tinted friezes, frescoes, and hand-stenciled designs decorated the walls, and medallions with paintings representing early Nebraska agriculture, music, art, oratory, and literature graced the sides and top of the stage. The drop curtain featured a representation of the Biblical story of the finding of Moses, with an additional scene of the Vatican; the second curtain depicted the entrance to Rheims cathedral. The auditorium also featured a motion picture screen and projector to show educational films to entertain and instruct the students. The auditorium was two stories high with a balcony on the second floor and rooms for the music department on the third level above it. Also in 1917 the manual training classes expanded into a large 129-by-20-foot basement room excavated under the south wing.

By December 1920, 9,678 students had matriculated: 1,295 had earned diplomas, 914 received life certificates, 788 obtained elementary certificates, and 51 acquired AB degrees. The teaching faculty had increased from the original 21 to 41 plus the addition of administrative positions. The initial value of the campus had risen from $91,000 to $755,600 with an expected appropriation of $240,000 for 1921.

❖ COMMERICAL CLUB

Appreciating the importance of the Normal School to the community, the Kearney Commercial Club organized an auto tour and picnic for 1,000 students and faculty in 1917. Riding in 200 automobiles furnished by Kearney citizens, the group toured the 1733 Ranch, paraded down Central Avenue accompanied by the Industrial School boys' band, and picnicked on potato salad and 2,000 roast beef sandwiches at Kearney Country Club. The Commercial Club believed that the school was "one of the pillars of this growing community," and the businessmen wanted in every way possible "to boost the institution and make the student visitors feel that their presence here is desirable."

❖ ACADEMICS

In the first decades of the twentieth century, in addition to increased interest in a more diverse curriculum, Americans became concerned about improving educational methods to create better qualified teachers. Initially the Normal School offered a two-year degree, requiring classes in teaching methods as well as mathematics, geography, English, and psychology. Students could also choose from electives in the sciences, including zoology and chemistry as well as the arts, such as drawing and music.

ANNA V. JENNINGS

Anna V. Jennings organized the first library at the Normal School in 1905 on the third floor of the Administration building and served as the school's head librarian for the next 34 years. During World War I she organized a drive to send 1,200 books and seven boxes of magazines to military camps. Given a leave of absence and then forced to retire in 1939 because of faculty reductions, her disappointed ghost is alleged to still haunt the library. Jennings was honored for her service to the school in 1986 when the Anna V. Jennings Room was dedicated on the second floor of the Calvin T. Ryan Library.

Students pay attention in orderly rows

◆ CARRIE E. LUDDEN

Carrie E. Ludden, a student in the first class to attend the Normal School, joined the staff as a laboratory assistant in 1906, and for the next 48 years she worked in the biology department. She was elected secretary of the Alumni Association in 1911 and served in that office until 1926, and then intermittently until 1957. During World War II she wrote letters to all KSTC servicemen. At the time of her retirement in 1953, she had served the college longer than any other faculty member, and in 1961 a new women's dormitory, built on the former site of Green Terrace Hall, was named in her honor.

Students could enter the Normal School directly after eighth-grade graduation from either rural or city schools. Preparatory studies were available in all departments. The general course of study spanned five years, including three secondary and two college years. Area teachers who held first grade certificates or students who had completed two years of high school could enter the teacher training class. Upon the completion of this course of study, students received elementary state certificates good for three years; upon completion of the general courses, students earned state life certificates. The school also awarded diplomas upon the completion of the two-year college course. A special rural diploma would qualify the holder to become a principal of a rural or town school, a county superintendent, or a high school normal training teacher. In addition, special supervisor certificates could be earned for areas such as domestic science, music, physical culture, art, and manual training, and the school issued a three-year commercial diploma from the Department of Commerce.

In 1906 a typical first-year student took 18 credits the first semester: arithmetic (5), geography (4), grammar (5), and U.S. history (4). During the second semester, a student normally registered for bookkeeping (3), physiology (3), agriculture (4), civics (4), and reading (5), for a total of 19 credits. A normal day for a student, like Clara Finkwiler from Fullerton in the teacher training class, included the following: 8:00 geography; 9:30 observation; 10:45 arithmetic; 1:30 civics; and 3:45 U.S. History. Two hundred credits—160 required hours and 40 electives—were necessary for graduation. Clara's tuition was free, except for a one–time matriculation fee of $5. She paid from 40¢ to 75¢ per week for a room and board, and $1 for textbook rental.

First graduating class

In May 1906, 17 women formed the first graduating class from the Normal School program with 28 women in the teacher training class. They began the tradition of presenting a Senior Pedagogical Thesis to the public during graduation week. Among the speakers were Selma Reasoner, who spoke on "Educational Values," and Helen A. Hicks, who explained "The Theory of Manual Training." The Kearney Opera House hosted the first commencement where the Normal School orchestra played "America's Pride" by Scotti and "March from Forbidden Lands" by Chopin. Guided by Professor Carrie Ludden, these first graduates chose Mildred Johnson as president of the newly formed Alumni Association, and 17 members joined together "to promote in every proper way the interest of the Normal School, and to foster among its members a sentiment of regard for one another and attachment of their alma mater."

Art classes were an intrinsic part of the curriculum from the founding of the Normal School. Marion C. Smith, one of the original faculty members, created the program with three objectives: to increase appreciation for art, to develop skill in art, and to train art teachers. History, too, succeeded because of the efforts of a single professor, C. N. Anderson, who taught the entire history curriculum and remained on the faculty from 1905 until 1929.

The Division of Language and Literature boasted three English teachers, George Porter, Mary Crawford, and Edith L. Robbins, plus two foreign language teachers, Alma Hosic, German, and Gertrude Gardner, Latin. By 1917 four full-time and one part-time teacher taught 8 secondary and 22 collegiate English courses. In addition to literature appreciation, composition, and dramatic expression, new courses in advanced speaking and the familiar essay helped students learn how to gather, classify, and evaluate information and begin scholarly investigation. The department also offered courses in journalism, dramatic composition, stage craft, pageantry, public speaking, rural school problems in English, and business English. The English Club, which encouraged original creative writing, formed in 1910.

To help develop the forensics program, clubs, such as the men's Emanon Debating Society, organized in 1905, and the women's Aspasian Debating Society, started in 1906. In 1908 the two rival societies debated each other, with the judges voting unanimously that the women were equal sparring partners with the men. The first triangular debates were held with Hastings College and Grand Island College in 1916, but the Kearney teams did not win a decision. However, when Professor Ralph Noyer took charge of the debates in 1917, arguing the issue, "Resolved: That immigration should be further restricted by means of a literacy test," the results proved more positive. The coed teams for the affirmative against Grand Island and the

❖ COURSE
OFFERINGS

CLARENCE A.
MURCH

Educator, poet, sportsman, and Kearney businessman Clarence A. Murch established the Kearney Business College on the fourth floor of the Kearney Opera House in 1898. In 1904 he closed the business college to join the staff of the Normal School, and in 1905 he was named principal of the Department of Commerce. Although Murch died just 4½ years later, it was not before he had time to finish writing the school's first "color song," now the UNK Alma Mater.

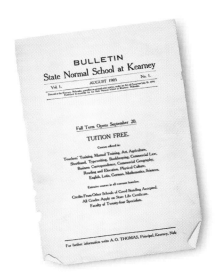

◆ RALPH W. NOYER

Less than two months after a traveling production company staged two Shakespearean plays at the Normal School, Professor Ralph W. Noyer, head of the English department and the school's debate coach from 1916 to 1922, decided to stage his own Shakespearean production. On July 18, 1917, as many as 1,200 students and townspeople arrived at the new auditorium despite great heat to watch the school's first showing of *Hamlet*, which lasted four hours. Three years later, Noyer delighted Normal School audiences with *The Merry Wives of Windsor*.

Dramatics Club

negative against Hastings both won by unanimous verdicts from the judges. First held in the chapel and later moved to the new auditorium, the early debates were very popular and successful, sometimes drawing standing-room-only audiences.

Drama also developed through student organizations. The Dramatics Club, later renamed the Theater Arts League, organized in 1908 and produced more than 40 major productions during the Normal School years. With the goal of giving each member an opportunity to perform, the club presented several short plays each year.

Music played an essential part in most Nebraska State Normal School gatherings, including chapel, convocations, athletic events, holiday activities, and commencement. The men's Glee Club, organized in 1906 with 21 voices, and the women's Nordicean Glee Club, founded in 1907 and 30 voices strong, sang separately and combined in a chorus to present at least three full-length concerts a year at Easter, Christmas, and commencement. The first production of a choral group was a part of Handel's *Messiah* at the Easter chapel service in 1907. In 1919 the Nordiceans changed their name to the St. Cecilians.

With only eight members in the orchestra in 1905, ten in 1906, and six in 1907, including the director, English professor George N. Porter, the orchestra program at Kearney developed slowly. Moreover, since Porter also organized the band in 1908 and directed it, played clarinet in the orchestra, sang baritone as a soloist with the chorus, and coached the football team, orchestra practice could not be scheduled until after Thanksgiving. Nevertheless, the group performed on many notable occasions, such as the first commencement in 1906. Professor Benjamin H. Patterson took over the orchestra in 1910. By 1911 the music department had grown sufficiently to perform the comic opera *Sinbad the Sailor*, directed by Grace Steadman, as well as other musicals and operettas.

The domestic science program, begun in 1909 by Marion Williams Wellers, occupied a cottage that served as a laboratory on 24th Street near the campus. Taught by Wellers from 1909 to 1924, women studied the composition, production, manufacturing, nutrition, and cooking of food as well as dressmaking, millinery, textiles, and pattern drafting. They also learned about home construction, heating, lighting, and plumbing. The program was renamed the Department of Household Science and Management in 1917.

The first manual training courses—such as woodworking and agriculture—taught by A. J. Mercer, met in the heating plant and were open to men and women. By 1914 it officially became the Department of Manual Training, and Charles Wellers replaced Professor Mercer, who continued teaching in the geography and agriculture departments. The department moved to the Administration building in 1916, and the faculty grew to include Professor L. E. Burton in 1917 and Professor Otto C. Olsen in 1919.

The agricultural program, established to conduct field research, teach students how to manage farms, and give would-be rural teachers an understanding of farm life, became another important area of study at the Normal School. A small farm equipped with used machinery and conveniently adjacent to Collins School served as a laboratory where student teachers could work both on the farm and in the school at the same location. The agriculture program expanded rapidly, and by 1916 the Rural Club involved 220 members, the largest organization on campus with 18 more members than the Recreation Club.

Professor Leslie B. Sipple developed the rural education department in 1916. In addition to offering college pedagogy classes, the department used country schools in Buda, Glenwood, Collins, and Victor as training schools.

Working on the school farm

OTTO C. OLSEN

Otto C. Olsen, whose campus career spanned 38 years from 1919 to 1957, graduated from the Normal School in 1919 and joined the staff of the industrial training department the same year. From 1939 until his retirement in 1957, he served as chairman of the vocational arts division. Before that, he served as chairman of the industrial arts department for 21 years. Under his direction, the school became one of the first in the nation to offer instruction in driver education. In 1961 the Vocational Arts building, constructed in 1954, was renamed the Otto C. Olsen Vocational Arts building.

◆ **GEORGE N. PORTER**

George N. Porter organized many of the Normal School's first extracurricular activities. As a professor of English literature, he advised the first English Club and coached the first men's debate team, the Emanon Debating Society. He also coached the first football team, directed the first band and orchestra, and performed as a baritone soloist for the school chorus. In 1905 Porter's commitment to the football team forced him to postpone orchestra practice for the Christmas concert until after Thanksgiving. Porter later left the school to become the principal of Garfield High School in Seattle, Washington.

Professor and Mrs. R. W. Powell later taught rural education. By 1925 seven Nebraska rural schools were affiliated with the program. The Normal School transported the student teachers to the training schools, and the schools, in turn, hired teachers from those recommended by the Normal School.

The psychology program, headed by W. A. Clark, maintained a high profile throughout the state. While still employed by Peru Normal, Clark participated in a 1900 symposium on the History of Education in Nebraska at the 42nd Annual Meeting of the State Teachers Association in Lincoln. In 1910 he addressed the annual meeting of the Nebraska State Institute on "General Preparation of Instructors." In addition, he served on the statewide committee that set the standards for major and minor requirements for first grade certificates. By 1915 course options in the psychology program expanded, and Charles Emile Benson, a University of Nebraska graduate and student of Professor Harry Kirke Wolfe (who established the first psychology laboratory in the Midwest) implemented the study of the psychology of child development at Kearney Normal.

To meet the needs of Normal School students, especially teachers returning to upgrade their certificates or specialize in other departments, the summer school program increasingly enlarged its offerings. By 1917 classes included Spanish, German, French, juvenile literature, sheet metal work, industrial geography, and quantitative analysis as well as the usual core courses. Students were met at the railway station and transported for free by bus to the campus to register. In 1917 enrollment swelled to 900, despite men registering for the draft, and nine additional faculty were hired for the summer term. By 1921 summer enrollment topped 1,300, creating an emergency housing crisis, and President George Martin asked Kearney residents to "throw open their homes" to students.

REORGANIZATION ◆

As the campus expanded physically, a major administrative reorganization of departments became necessary. In 1914 the Normal Board mandated that the number of departments should be limited and unified, with each having a head and one to two assistants. Department heads were required to have a bachelor's degree, one year of teachers training, and two or more years of successful teaching experience. Kearney Normal established the following departments: geography, history, civics, English, mathematics, physical sciences, natural sciences, Latin or ancient languages, German or modern languages, reading, education, physical education, training for teaching. The classification of special departments included business training, agriculture, manual arts (manual training, domestic training, art of drawing), and music. Another major change took place in 1920 when the school switched from the semester to the quarter system.

Dean of faculty M. R. Snodgrass, acting president after the removal of A. O. Thomas in 1913, issued supervisor certificates in domestic science, commercial education, public school music, and expression. In 1914 he established the Department of Instrumental Music, whose faculty salaries were based on a percentage of fees collected for music lessons. In addition, he hired Charles D. Wellers to institute and teach manual training as well as assist in the athletic department.

In 1911 the Normal School announced that students would be able to take 20 additional hours in education and another 60 hours of specialization (major and minor) to earn a bachelor of education degree, which would be equivalent to the four-year baccalaureate degree awarded by colleges and universities. In 1918, 20 seniors received the degree.

President Thomas summarized the academic values of the institution in 1912, stating that faculty "brought as many different ideals and educational creeds to the new institution as there were members in the faculty. Brick and stone and mortar and students and teachers do not make a school. It is necessary to develop an institutional ideal or unity of purpose." State Examining Boards visiting the campus consistently praised the standards of the Normal School.

❖ SOCIAL ACTIVITIES

The years between 1900 and 1920 were a time of growth and change for the United States. Although the turn of the century was considered the Progressive Era, and rumblings of women's suffrage and women's rights could be heard in the distance, the traditional Victorian gender roles and codes of behavior still prevailed at Kearney's Normal School.

In the early years of the Normal School, the administration set strict codes for behavior, not only in the classroom, but also in the community. The student handbook admonished: "Don't brag, skip classes, loaf in the halls, talk too much, talk about yourself or forget the chapel hour. Do write home every week, be quiet in the halls, pay your dues promptly, attend church every Sunday, learn the college yell and wear the college colors." Teachers maintained classroom desks in orderly rows and could drop students from the rolls after three absences. Loitering, congregating, laughing, or loud talking in the halls were not allowed. As for social life, parties and school entertainment could only be scheduled for Friday and Saturday evenings, but dancing on campus was prohibited. As a result, students often organized unchaperoned dancing parties off campus where "regrettable instances" occurred, causing the Board to reconsider holding dances on campus. Pool halls in the community were off limits, and students caught in them were often suspended.

ALICE M. ROBINSON

Alice M. Robinson earned an AB from KSTC in 1919. She later received her AM from the University of California in 1922 and completed graduate work at Columbia and Syracuse universities beginning in 1924. In 1927 she returned to Kearney and joined the KSTC faculty as a Latin professor. In 1934 she taught 23 Latin classes. The following year she became the school's dean of women. In 1954 Robinson joined the English faculty. She married Fred McCready, a Kearney attorney, in 1957 and retired in 1960.

Just as the administration regulated student behavior, they also set the policy for proper attire. For school and dress occasions, young women normally wore white blouses with high, buttoned collars and narrow, floor-length, dark skirts, and they pulled their long hair into neat buns or chignons on top or at the back of their heads. Men sported dark suits, stiffly starched white shirts, and long ties. At the beginning of the 1900s, both fashionable men and women wore long bow ties. In the physical education classes, women donned black bloomers and white middy blouses.

Students at Kearney Normal School balanced their academic lives with social activities. Green Terrace was the center for entertainment on the campus and hosted the first social event in the history of the Normal School on July 14, 1905, when the Normal faculty formally met the citizens of Kearney. On October 30, 1905, Green Terrace held the first Halloween party with jack-o'-lanterns eerily illuminating the reception room. Students attempted to outdo each other by dressing up like corpses, ghosts, and mourners and decorating their rooms with skulls, bones, coffins, and snakes. For 10¢ guests could enter the Chambers of Horror. Booths with food for sale and fortune tellers offered entertainment in the reception room until 9:30 when a parade of young women entered and unmasked, revealing their identities.

First social event in the history of the Normal School

Young Women's Christian Association

MARION SMITH

Marion Smith attended Emporia State Teachers College, the University of Nebraska, the Pennsylvania Academy of Fine Arts, the Art Institute of Chicago, and the Handicraft Guild of Minneapolis before being appointed to the Normal School faculty in 1905. As the school's first art teacher, she was often credited with helping to bring art to Kearney in its initial years of growth. She is known mostly for the portraits of Native Americans that she made on trips to the Rosebud Reservation in South Dakota; a sample of her work is housed at the Museum of Nebraska Art. Smith was among the last original faculty members to retire in 1943.

The first social groups organized on campus included the Young Women's Christian Association in 1905, followed by the Young Men's Christian Association the next year; both held meetings in the reception room of the dormitory every Sunday afternoon. Although these groups were mainly social, sponsoring receptions or parties a few times a year, they also held devotional meetings. Around 1910 the Catholic Club began, and six years later it hosted the national convention of the Catholic Students Association of America. The Emanon Literary Society also scheduled Saturday evening programs at the dormitory.

Professor Grace Steadman organized the Juanita Girls sorority in 1910, and Sigma Theta Phi organized in 1915. Fraternities, too, began forming: Phi Tau Gamma chartered in 1915 and the Caledonians in 1916. Other social organizations during this period included the Longfellows Club for men at least six feet tall, the Tegner Society for students of Swedish, and later Danish and Norwegian, ancestry, the Sodalistis Latina, Der Deutsche Verein, the Froebel Kindergarten Bund, the Dramatics Club, the Culture Club, the English Club, Episol Beta (physical development) and the Freshman, Sophomore, Junior, and Senior Class organizations.

To document these notable events, the yearbook, the *Blue and Gold,* began preserving campus history in 1908. The first biennial volume, containing 100 pages, recorded major campus events, musings on daily student life, brief histories of organizations, and portraits of the seniors and faculty as well as photos of the school. Further editions followed intermittently until 1923, then annually with the exception of 1945 during the war.

On December 2, 1910, the school newspaper, the *Antelope*–taking its name from the new mascot–launched weekly publication. Completely supported by advertising, nearly half of the paper was filled with ads during the

John Stryker

Early-era photographer John Stryker, hired to teach penmanship at the Normal School in 1909, recorded much of the institution's early history. His interest in photography took hold in earnest when he acquired a Kodak camera and began doing publicity work for the Normal School in 1916. From 1915 to 1919, Stryker preserved much of Kearney and the surrounding area on film and took pictures for the Normal School annual. When he retired in 1919, he was replaced at the Normal School by his wife, Elsie Johnson, a former penmanship supervisor at North Platte. After one of Stryker's rodeo pictures was used by Eastman Kodak for its national advertising campaign in 1920, Stryker went on to become a rodeo and then a circus announcer. He announced 52 consecutive shows for the Ringling Brothers in New York before going on the road with the troupe.

first years of publication. The Antelope covered campus affairs, such as upcoming events, class notes, inspirational and humorous anecdotes, and it praised the school's accomplishments. Later the student Single Tax helped support production, allowing the newspaper to reach out to high schools and alumni in addition to Normal School students.

World War I ❖ The entry of the United States into World War I in 1917 changed the focus of the campus, causing a flurry of support from faculty and students alike. In April, L Company shipped off to Europe; among these first troops were 8 Kearney Normal students. By December a total of 30 students from the fall term alone had departed for war. In addition, the school granted excused absences for 18 men to help with the corn harvest and husking, leaving less than 100 male students at the school.

The library displayed information on Red Cross relief activities, including directions on knitting for the troops, and in conjunction with the American Library Association, sent 1,200 books to military camps. The German department removed several books from the library and the curriculum that contained pictures of the German royalty or instilled in the minds of American language students "a love for the German ideals." Meanwhile, campus groups organized fund-raising activities, such as pageants, concerts, and plays, and mailed care packages overseas. Marion Wellers's sewing class created more than 800 sweaters for the troops, about 200 hospital and refugee garments, and 7 quilts. Various groups and classes adopted orphans in France, with the class of 1917 accepting two. The Antelope published letters written by soldiers with connections to the school, who thanked students for their support.

The school also began offering a course in military drill, and although not mandatory, every enrolled young man signed up for it. A women's company formed as well. Wallace Reynolds, football coach and Spanish and Latin teacher who had gained experience in Mexico during the 1915 revolution, acted as the drill master. Two companies met five days a week for 30 minutes. In October 1918 the Student Army Training Corps was organized, and the government used the new gymnasium as a barracks. However, two months later, after Germany signed an armistice with the Allies and the war ended, the 71 members demobilized.

Three men from the Normal School were killed in action: Clarence M. Olsen, who was buried in France; Floyd Hedglin, who went down with the President Lincoln; and Chaplain W. H. J. Wilby, who died at sea.

Football team

From the start, athletics performed a vital role at the Kearney Normal School, despite inadequate facilities and humble beginnings. In October 1905 Wynfred E. Allen and A. J. Mercer organized an official football team. Only three of the students knew anything about the game, so they began with the rudiments. The Kearney High School team demolished them, and they ended the season scoreless with a 0-5-1 record against high school teams.

In 1906 the school completed a dirt field and grandstand where Thomas Hall now stands. It ran east-west with a small set of bleachers on the north and a board fence protecting it from 24th Street traffic on the south. The 1906 football team, coached by Allen, recorded a 3-4-2 season, scoring a total of 28 points. In 1907 George Porter took over coaching duties, and the team began playing colleges. Doane, the first college team they played, defeated them 18-0. The games were very informal. In a 1908 game, with the score 21-0 in favor of the Grand Island Business School, officials halted

❖ MEN'S SPORTS

Sports and grandstand

1907 men's and women's basketball

1915 football schedule

Fans watch football from the bleachers

1910 men's "base ball" team

1919 football team

1908 men's basketball team

Early men's tennis

◆ GEORGE VAN BUREN

George Van Buren coached every major sport at the Normal School, including football, basketball, baseball, and track, from 1910 to 1914. As a former all-around athlete at Cornell College in Iowa, he played on several championship teams before accepting the position of physical education instructor and director of athletics at Kearney. In his first year as head coach, he guided the football team to its first winning season. He led the baseball team to its first championship the following year. When Van Buren decided to leave the school in 1914, its position as an emerging power in state athletics had already been solidified.

play because several of the Normal School players had to report to their after-school jobs. By 1910 the team, coached by George Van Buren, had its first winning season, and by 1911 Kearney Normal competed predominantly against other colleges. That year they lost to the University of Nebraska by a score of 117-0. At the first Homecoming, held Thanksgiving weekend in 1915, Kearney lost to the Grand Island Baptists 17-19. The playing field was moved north of the present location of the library in 1916. The football team continued to struggle over the next two decades.

The basketball team also encountered obstacles on the road to winning seasons. Kearney Normal's first men's basketball team played during the 1906-7 season and was coached by Professor Allen. The team played both high school and college opponents and ended the season with a 2-2 record. When Professor A. J. Mercer became the coach in 1908, the team enjoyed a 4-2 record but played only high schools. In 1909 the basketball team added Doane College, Peru Normal, and Grand Island Business School to the schedule, ending the season with a 3-3-2 record. The following year the statistics took a dive, but the Kearney Normal men began competing against college teams like Cotner College, Doane College, Nebraska Wesleyan, and York College.

In the beginning, the men's basketball team had no place to practice except a classroom that they shared with the women's basketball team, and they played their games in the city armory. In 1911, under the direction of physical education professor Van Buren and manual training professor Mercer, the Normal School men built a 60-by-80-foot wood-frame gymnasium. The central area held a 40-by-60-foot dirt-floored basketball court encircled by a 75-yard cinder track. Spectators cheered the team from hay bales surrounding the court, and oil stoves furnished heat. Although the season in The Barn ended with a 2-11 record, by 1913 the men posted an 8-3 record. However, that was the last winning season until 1922.

The most successful of the early sports was "base ball," first coached by O. W. Neale. The team, playing local town teams during the summer on city fields, posted season records of 8-1 in 1905, 13-1 in 1906, 13-3 in 1907, and 10-6 in 1908. Van Buren guided the team to a championship in 1911, and they suffered only one losing season until the school suspended baseball in 1913-14 due to lack of funding. Harry Tollefsen began coaching in 1914, posting a losing season that year but a winning one the next. The baseball team organized again during the spring of 1917 but disbanded after the United States declared war on Germany since many of the athletes departed immediately for the service. World War I halted all baseball contests until a final game in 1920, coached by Hugo Outopalik. Kearney lost, and the school did not reinstate baseball until 1961.

Normal School men's "base ball" team

Men's track suffered a similar fate. Debuting in 1911 and coached by Van Buren, six men reported for the team that spring and the next. However, like baseball, the track team had to suspend practice in 1913-14, this time because of the school's financial problems. Although the size of the squad increased to nine men in 1914, finances and World War I caused the program to be suspended until the 1920s.

In 1905 women's athletics competed for headlines with the men, especially since a large majority of the students were women. In addition, the school was on the quarter system, and many of the male students worked in the fields during the fall and spring, attending class only during the winter sessions. Early in the fall term of 1905, Professor Allen organized a women's basketball team and scheduled five games. In March 1906 the first women's basketball game was held between Peru and Kearney at the armory. Burned-out light fuses delayed the game, but the score at halftime stood at 13–11. Three of Kearney's players had never played basketball before this year, and even Celia Hull, the tallest and best player for Kearney, could not prevent the 26-16 loss. After the game, the team held a reception in the chapel for the visiting team with a program of readings and music and served ambrosia in orange shells. The next year Professor H. O. Sutton acted as coach, and the team, with a Teddy Bear as a mascot, won four of their seven games.

By the team's third year, 1907-8, Professor Grace Hamer served as coach, and former basketball player, Lora Huntley, assisted her, leading the women to a 7-4 season. Huntley began coaching in 1908-9. Her team played against high schools from Minden, Hastings, Grand Island, and Kearney, and she ended her first year with a 4-1 record. Women's athletics disappeared as an

❖ **WOMEN'S SPORTS**

◆ CHARLES WARNER

In 1903 Charles Warner, the first speaker of the Nebraska Unicameral, led the effort to establish the Normal School in Kearney. A member of the Nebraska House of Representatives from 1901 to 1907, the Nebraska Senate from 1919 to 1937, and the Unicameral Legislature from 1937 to 1939, Warner ran for governor three times but was unsuccessful. He was elected lieutenant governor four times beginning in 1949. His son, Jerome Warner, surpassed his father's service in the legislature, serving as a state senator for 35 years. In 1989 the son of the Grand Old Man of Nebraska Politics introduced a bill making KSC part of the University of Nebraska system.

1907–8 women's basketball team

interscholastic activity in 1916 and were not reinstated until the 1960s. In 1910, however, a coed Tennis Club was organized, and members could play on three courts. Twelve women also formed a tennis club, calling themselves The Courtin' Club and swearing allegiance to each other off and on the court.

ATHLETIC ❖
ASSOCIATION

The first Athletic Association met in January 1909 to appoint yell committees. By 1911 the men of the school decided to organize a more official Athletic Association to "take charge of the athletics of the school." The next fall, the Normal School students assembled and decided to assess themselves $3 per year to support all student activities: literary organizations, lectures and entertainment, intercollegiate debates, the school paper, and athletics. The athletic

Coed Tennis Club

board applauded this decision, voted unanimously for the fee, and elected Norwin Holzmark as yell leader. Support for athletics would continue to grow with the campus.

With teams in all sports, the need for a mascot arose, and in 1910 the Normal School selected the antelope, for it symbolized "strength, swiftness and the ability to adapt to adverse conditions." Considering the early history of sports at Kearney, this was an appropriate choice.

In the first 1905 school bulletin, Dr. Thomas set forth the ideals of the Nebraska State Normal School at Kearney: "The real mission of the Normal school is to prepare the coming teacher that she will ever keep before her the fundamental law which declares that the real purpose of teaching is to kindle a glowing and lasting fire in the pupil's heart. Not merely to fill his head with facts but to develop characteristics, habits, methods of thought, feeling, and action." Throughout these early years, the leaders of the Kearney Normal School looked to the future, building not only firm foundations of stone and steel but a sound philosophy of education that would serve the institution and the state well in the following years.

❖ **CONCLUSION**

NEBRASKA STATE
TEACHERS COLLEGE
AT KEARNEY

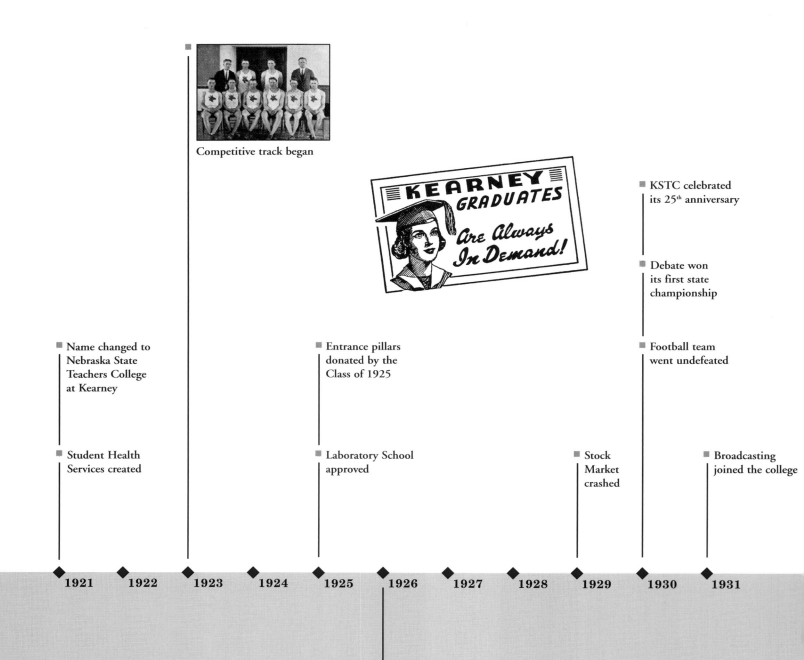

Competitive track began

KEARNEY GRADUATES
Are Always In Demand!

■ KSTC celebrated
its 25th anniversary

■ Debate won
its first state
championship

■ Name changed to
Nebraska State
Teachers College
at Kearney

■ Entrance pillars
donated by the
Class of 1925

■ Football team
went undefeated

■ Student Health
Services created

■ Laboratory School
approved

■ Stock
Market
crashed

■ Broadcasting
joined the college

◆ **1921**   ◆ **1922**   ◆ **1923**   ◆ **1924**   ◆ **1925**   ◆ **1926**   ◆ **1927**   ◆ **1928**   ◆ **1929**   ◆ **1930**   ◆ **1931**

Laboratory school
■ completed

NEBRASKA STATE
TEACHERS COLLEGE
AT KEARNEY

Laboratory school renamed A.O.
Thomas Laboratory School

Mens Hall dedicated–first
dormitory built for men

■ First "Gridiron Queen"
elected – Patsy Hamer

■ Seventeen departments
reduced to eight

■ The Great Depression
(1933–1938)

■ A.O Thomas
Laboratory High
School closed

■ World War II
(1941–1945)

1932   1933   1934   1935   1936   1937   1938   1939   1940   1941   1942

Carnegie Grant added
500 art books and 2,000
■ reproductions to library

Herbert L. Cushing
■ became president

NEBRASKA STATE
TEACHERS COLLEGE
AT KEARNEY

1943

Former Officers Club building from
Kearney Air Base moved to campus to
serve as temporary student union

◼ First student union,
Kampus Kave, opened

◼ Drama League began
producing plays

◼ Korean Conflict
(1950–1953)

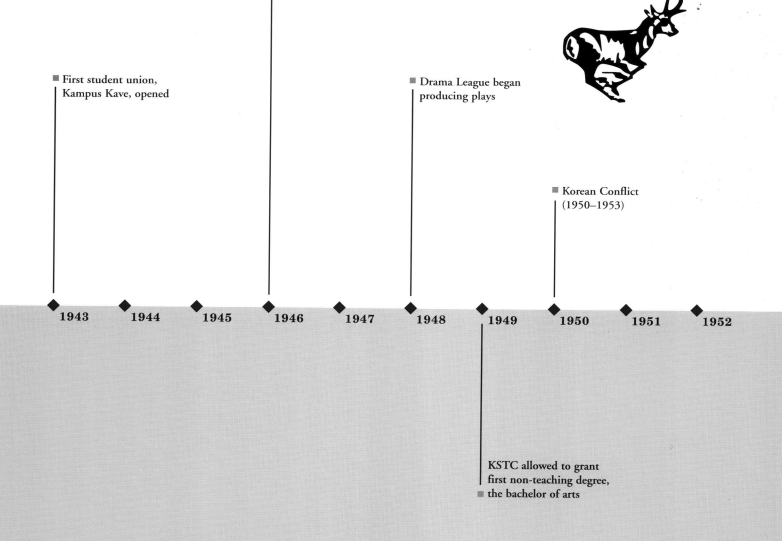

| 1943 | 1944 | 1945 | 1946 | 1947 | 1948 | 1949 | 1950 | 1951 | 1952 |

KSTC allowed to grant
first non-teaching degree,
◼ the bachelor of arts

◼ 34

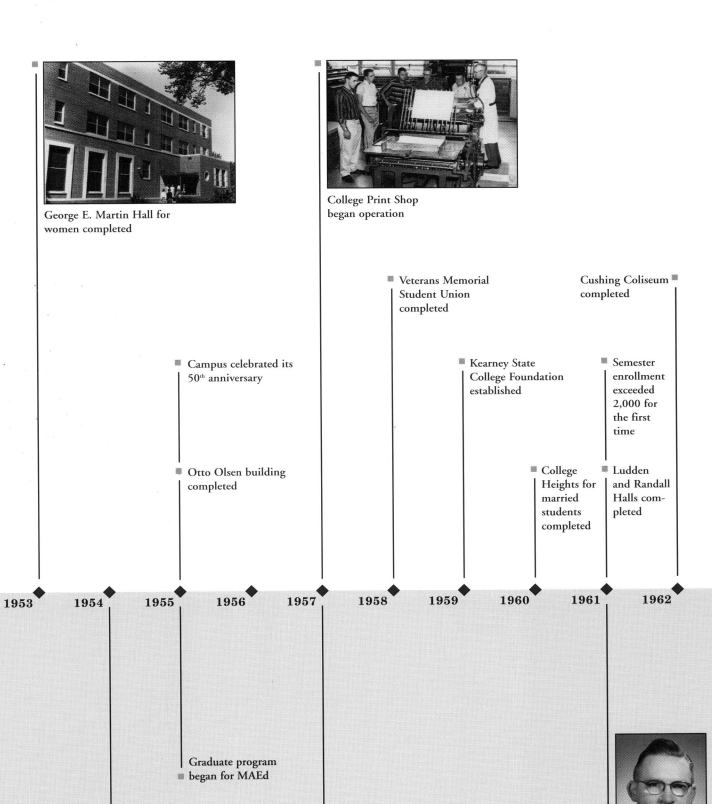

George E. Martin Hall for
women completed

College Print Shop
began operation

Veterans Memorial
Student Union
completed

Cushing Coliseum
completed

Campus celebrated its
50th anniversary

Kearney State
College Foundation
established

Semester
enrollment
exceeded
2,000 for
the first
time

Otto Olsen building
completed

College
Heights for
married
students
completed

Ludden
and Randall
Halls com-
pleted

1953   **1954**   **1955**   **1956**   **1957**   **1958**   **1959**   **1960**   **1961**   **1962**

Graduate program
began for MAEd

Program of basic
studies created

First graduate degrees
awarded

Milton J. Hassel
became president

CHAPTER TWO
1921-1963

❖ In 1921 Nebraska State Normal School at Kearney officially changed its name to
Nebraska State Teachers College at Kearney, and the State Normal Board authorized
the college to grant baccalaureate degrees in the liberal arts in 1949, eliminating the
requirement that all students complete a teacher certification program.

Nebraska State Teachers College at Kearney

❖ TRANSFORMATIONS

T he years between 1921 and 1963 heralded greater transformations than even the founders of Nebraska State Normal School at Kearney could have imagined. When George E. Martin, former head of the English department and dean of teacher training, was appointed president in 1919, he led the institution to the next academic level, one that would last more than 40 years. Martin was convinced that if the school was designated a college that granted bachelor's degrees, more students would remain the full four years instead of discontinuing their education at two. Moreover, educational leaders believed that although the teachers in the elementary grades were well-grounded in pedagogy, the high schools had been dominated by people who had no training or professional interest in education. Many believed that a two-year course for certification tended to cheapen the teaching profession. Elevating teaching to a professional level with the awarding of a bachelor's degree from a four-year college would raise the standards for teachers, attract better candidates for the state's high schools, and lure more students into entering "the greatest of all professions." Further, the prestige of the institution's new status as a college would attract better faculty, for it would not be considered simply an extension of secondary school.

In 1921 Nebraska State Normal School at Kearney officially changed its name to Nebraska State Teachers College at Kearney (later unofficially shortened to KSTC), and the State Normal Board authorized the college to grant baccalaureate degrees in the liberal arts in 1949, eliminating the requirement that all students complete a teacher certification program. This allowed the education faculty to focus its energy on students preparing to enter the teaching profession. On March 25 after unanimously passing both the lower house of the Nebraska Legislature and the Senate, Governor Samuel R. McKelvie signed bills 216 and 223, constituting a landmark in Nebraska educational history. The first bill empowered the board of education to prescribe the subjects taught by schools of education, while the second not only specified which certificates, diplomas, and degrees could be conferred upon students completing the various courses but changed the names of the four Nebraska State Normal Schools.

Although requirements for the old certificates and diplomas remained the same, the bill added that the Board of Education of State Normal Schools would grant any student completing the four-year collegiate course a bachelor of arts degree and a first grade state certificate entitling the holder to teach in any of the schools in the state without further examination for three years.

Harold L. Ahrendts

When President Herbert Cushing hired Harold L. Ahrendts to direct the forensics program in 1943, he hoped to emphasize speech "as much as some schools emphasize athletics," and within four years, three of Ahrendts's students had qualified for national forensics competitions. His students sometimes traveled 10,000 miles in a single season to attend as many as 15 tournaments across the country. A total of nine students reached the finals of the National Interstate Oratorical Contest, winning two national championships, two third places, one fourth place, and one fifth. Between 1940 and 1963 KSTC won 77 first places at the Nebraska Intercollegiate Forensic Association Tournament (which excluded the University of Nebraska) in debate, extemporaneous speaking, oratory, and peace oratory.

President Cushing in his office

The stock market crash in 1929 and the resulting Depression intensified funding struggles that had been developing on the campus over the years. Little construction took place at KSTC in the 1930s and 1940s. In 1939 severe budget restrictions forced the closing of the A. O. Thomas Laboratory High School, a 20 percent reduction in faculty, and a reorganization of the 17 departments into 7—all without a drop in enrollment. During President Martin's term of office, from 1919 to 1936, college enrollment grew from approximately 305 to 825, yet the number of faculty only rose from 36 to 55. In addition, a rift occurred between the campus and the community when a few businessmen unsuccessfully petitioned to reduce faculty salaries since some of the teachers were making more money than they were.

In 1935 President Martin's health began to fail, but he continued his duties until his final hospitalization in the last few weeks of his life when doctors discovered that he was also suffering from the final stages of cancer. Upon Martin's death, Herbert L. Cushing assumed the office of president on November 1, 1936. He had previously served as deputy state superintendent in the State Department of Education. Cushing, whose appointment divided the Normal Board, held the longest tenure in the college history, from 1936 to 1961.

The involvement of the United States in World War II (1941-1945) further devastated the campus. On December 8, 1941, the students of KSTC, as well as all American students, listened as President Roosevelt spoke about the war. The college granted leaves for military service to Professors Roland Welch of the commerce department, Durfee Larson of social sciences, and Robertson Strawn of fine arts. Students withdrew from classes daily, departing for the armed forces or defense work. The 1940s brought the war to Kearney's doorstep when it became home to the Kearney Army Air Field, dominating the city's way of life.

Enrollment shrank even more because of the growing teacher shortage, allowing students to teach with temporary credentials. Prewar enrollment in 1940 totaled 823; the following year it dropped to 369; by 1944 only 243 registered for classes with women making up 75 percent of the student body; and during the last war year, numbers increased slightly to 425. However, at the end of World War II, enrollment increased rapidly, and by 1947 it again rose to 786. After the Kearney air base closed in 1949 and peace resumed in the 1950s, returning men and women from the service flocked to Kearney.

The Korean Conflict (1950-1953) again drained the campus, dropping the enrollment to 628 students in 1953 with only 70 seniors. However, 294 freshmen enrolled, their numbers boosted by 58 veterans of World War II and the Korean Conflict, who were taking advantage of the new Veterans Readjustment Assistance Act of 1952. Seven of them were disabled. Enrollments climbed again, and the campus added new dormitories, a classroom building, plus a second heating plant east of the current West Center. Students helped bear the burden of this expansion, purchasing their own books for the first time in 1956 because of the large expense in the distribution and furnishing of texts.

❖ **WARS AND AFTERMATH**

William E. Bruner

William E. Bruner joined the KSTC staff in 1932 and served as chairman of the biological sciences division for the next 40 years. Considered an expert on midland grasses, he continued to teach biology even after his retirement in 1962. Eventually, however, Bruner moved to Portland, Oregon, to work in the field of plant biology. On September 30, 1965, the cornerstone was laid for the William E. Bruner Hall of Science, and the building was formally dedicated on April 26, 1967.

Students in front of Administration building

Herbert L. Cushing

Herbert L. Cushing assumed the presidency of KSTC in 1936 after working as deputy state superintendent in the Nebraska State Department of Education. During his tenure as president—the longest in school history—the college expanded to include a liberal arts degree option, a graduate program in education, and a $1.3 million coliseum that now bears Cushing's name. Upon his retirement in 1961, a special "Cushing Day" was declared in the president's honor. The school's new coliseum was dedicated on February 11, 1962, and on February 28, Cushing died of a heart attack. That same year Cushing was named along with Calvin T. Ryan as the third recipient of the college's Distinguished Service Award.

President Hassel

Throughout and following the war years, the college developed academically as well, appointing in 1951 H. G. Stout as the first dean of instruction, whose duties included the administration of the new graduate program in 1955. Each participating department developed courses to be used in this advanced degree program, a master's in education. In 1957, 50 students were enrolled in the graduate program, and the first master's degrees were granted to Donald Briggs, Robert Lundt, and Gladys Rose. Both Rose (art) and Briggs (journalism and English) joined the KSTC faculty upon graduation. Because of the growth in the graduate program, in 1958 the college appointed Myron Holm director of graduate studies; he occupied the position until 1969.

In 1961 Cushing reached the mandatory retirement age after 25 years of service. During his tenure, the campus experienced many changes. Upon his arrival in 1936, the college had 5 buildings, 40 faculty members, and over 800 students. When he retired, it had grown to 14 buildings, 105 faculty and staff, and 2,021 students. The State Normal Board selected Milton J. Hassel, a 1941 KSTC graduate, to succeed President Cushing in 1961. His appointment marked the first time that a college faculty committee assisted in the selection of a candidate for that position.

KEARNEY ❖ Kearney expanded along with the campus during these significant years with the census figures increasing steadily: 7,702 in 1920; 8,552 in 1930; 9,440 in 1940; 12,115 in 1950; and 14,210 in 1960. The rise of the automobile became a powerful social and economic force throughout this period. In 1921 one in five Kearney families owned a car, and the development of the Lincoln Highway, now Highway 30, linked Kearney to both ends of the state and nation, making it more accessible for shoppers, farmers, businessmen, and students. In 1963 Interstate 80 was constructed, bringing new residential, commercial, and public development to the city. Throughout the Normal School years, students arrived by carriage and by railway; during the early days of KSTC, students could drive themselves to college on the Lincoln Highway at 35 mph; and 40 years later, they could speed to their classes at 75 mph on the interstate.

Downtown Kearney 1927

View of downtown Kearney 1954

❖ **NEW BUILDINGS**

As campus facilities expanded, so did the learning opportunities offered to the students. In 1925 a laboratory school was approved at a cost of $85,000 to encourage enrollment in the four-year education programs. The school provided prospective teachers, supervisors, and school administrators the opportunity to study teaching under actual conditions. At the beginning, the college had difficulty finding even 20 children to participate, but once the new building was ready for occupancy on November 29, 1926, the classrooms filled, especially since tuition was free and the college offered one of the first kindergartens in the state and the only one in Kearney for many years.

The laboratory school provided a state-of-the-art facility. Classrooms to seat 20 to 30 children were 22 by 28 feet with 12-foot ceilings. Architects designed the rooms so that the windows, equal to approximately one-fourth the size of the room, would permit light to enter only from the rear and left side "in accordance with the latest scientific investigation." Each class included a conference room for the "critic

Case Hall

teacher" and the "practice teacher" to consult. The west end of the first floor housed the kindergarten suite that would accommodate 60 children. Students and faculty requested in 1932 that the building be named in honor of the first president, and it became the A. O. Thomas Laboratory School.

Residence halls also became a priority as the campus grew. Because of rising student numbers, the first residence hall for 180 freshman women was constructed in 1930 on the northeast corner of the campus. Named Eva J. Case Hall after one of the institution's original faculty members, everyone called it a 90-day wonder because workmen erected it during three summer months. The entire structure, except for doors and stair railings, was made of steel and concrete, unusual for the time and praised for its innovation.

Furnishings in a typical room included two single beds that folded into a closet, a dresser, two desks, two chairs, a rocking chair, and lavatory facilities. The bathrooms, two per floor, each contained two bathtubs and two showers. Laundry tubs were provided for the girls as well as space in the basement for hanging their clothes and for ironing. Green Terrace was eventually converted into efficiency apartments for women.

Little construction took place during the 1930s, and that was made possible only through federal funds from the Public Works Administration. One improvement was the paving of sidewalks and the circular drive around the Administration building. In addition, a federal grant provided $175,500 to help construct Mens Hall in 1939, the first residence hall for men. Considered "conservatively modern" in

Mens Hall interior

Mens Hall

**Miriam
Eckhardt Drake**

Miriam Eckhardt Drake joined the KSTC faculty in 1925 as a teacher of English and speech as well as the director of college plays and sponsor of the Theater Arts League. She taught full-time, part-time, or on a substitute basis and directed numerous plays, pageants, and faculty shows for 46 years. She directed 18 plays—more than anyone else at the time. In her first seven years, she supervised 24 major productions; her last was the musical *Vagabond King* in 1932. Drake retired in 1971 and in 1976 became the first woman to be awarded the school's Distinguished Service Award. In 1980 the theater in the Fine Arts Building was named the Miriam Drake Theater.

design for its time, the building had rounded corners and featured glass brick in the walls of the reception room and the dining hall alcoves. The cafeteria moved from Green Terrace to the east wing on the first floor of Mens Hall, and the former cafeteria became faculty lounges. Following World War II, the second- and third-floor lounges were converted into rooms to accommodate more students.

With the anticipated return of World War II soldiers, the State Normal Board secured 20 buildings donated by the federal government. The college moved the barracks from the air bases at Fairmont and Scribner to the northwest part of

♦ **Patsy Hamer**

In 1935 Patsy Hamer was voted KSTC's first Gridiron Queen. The idea for a football queen began during a 13-6 loss to traditional school rival Peru. Between downs, one of the KSTC players suggested that a queen might help the team play more "inspired football." Coach "Pop" Klein immediately sent a wire to Case Hall, Green Terrace Hall, the Sigma house, and several other places in Kearney, declaring that any girl who made it to Peru before the game ended would stand a "good chance" of becoming queen. Later that month, the K Club selected Hamer, a freshman and yell leader, as one of the first candidates. She was selected queen by a vote of the entire student body during convocation on November 26 of that year.

Vets Village

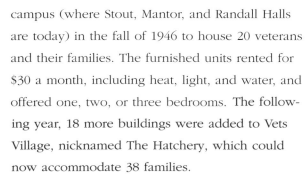

Otto C. Olsen building

campus (where Stout, Mantor, and Randall Halls are today) in the fall of 1946 to house 20 veterans and their families. The furnished units rented for $30 a month, including heat, light, and water, and offered one, two, or three bedrooms. The following year, 18 more buildings were added to Vets Village, nicknamed The Hatchery, which could now accommodate 38 families.

In 1955 classes opened in the new $770,000 Otto C. Olsen Vocational Arts building that housed the industrial arts, vocational home economics, and commerce departments. For the first time in 40 years, all sections of vocational arts could be taught under one roof. In addition to classrooms, the building featured a large food laboratory, a textile room, vocational shops, a preschool laboratory for the new child development program, and a small auditorium for lectures, visual presentations, and style shows. An additional $50,000 provided new industrial arts equipment. Moveable, full-length partitions with glass panels separated the shop areas to eliminate noise disturbance, allow more light, and permit teachers to better supervise all areas. Exhaust systems on the ceiling and floors helped to eliminate dust. When vocational arts moved out of the

Administration building, the library gained essential space; it had grown from 7,000 books in 1912 to 43,000 in 1955 with the periodical list expanding from 100 to 225.

Since students needed to balance their academic lives with some social activities, the necessity for a student center arose. In September 1943 the first student union on campus held its formal opening in the basement of Mens Hall. The Kampus Kave featured an ice cream bar and soda fountain, tables for ping pong and cards, a dance floor, and several booths. Tempera paintings of campus life created in 1943 by Willard Dority, a KSTC student, decorated the walls. In the summer of 1948, the college moved an abandoned army officers club from Scribner, Nebraska, and a government warehouse from Sioux City, Iowa, to campus to provide a temporary student union.

Although the school initially planned to house a permanent student union in a proposed new coliseum, it built, instead, a one-story brick building, the Veterans Memorial Student Union, in 1958. The idea for the memorial originated with Lulu E. Wirt, a former education teacher, whose estate donated $1,000 to begin a fund to honor the 28 men from KSTC killed in action in World

Student Union

Student Union snack bar

Veterans Memorial Student Union

Jeanette Harrison

Judy Funkhouser

The only students at KSTC to win national championships during the school's golden age of forensics from 1940 to 1963 were Jeanette Harrison and Judy Funkhouser. In 1949 Harrison won the women's division of the annual Interstate Oratorical Association Contest at Northwestern University. Funkhouser won the same title in 1961 for her speech "File Under S," an oration about the growing problem of sex crimes.

Martin Hall

Stout Hall

Conrad Hall

College Heights

Ludden Hall

Randall Hall

War II. Students established the Buck-a-Month Club in 1945 for a building to commemorate both the living and the dead that would "honor the past yet build for the future." When completed, the union housed a snack bar that could serve 95 while a dining room capable of seating 600 also functioned as a venue for dances. A lobby off of the snack bar opened into a game room and television lounge area. Offices for the student council, the *Antelope*, the *Blue and Gold*, the union director, and the publicity director completed the building.

Dormitories dominated the new construction, and the campus added six new residence halls within eight years. Martin Hall was built in 1953 for female upperclassmen, who provided suggestions for its design and furnishing. Two new dorms—Stout Hall for men and Jennie Conrad Hall for women—were finished in the fall of 1957 and added rooms for 210 more students. Conrad later housed the Office of Residential and Greek Life. College Heights for married students, completed in 1960, replaced Vets Village and featured 72 one-bedroom apartments and 36 efficiency units in three separate, T-shaped buildings that overlooked Kearney Lake north of the campus.

After the original Green Terrace was razed in 1959, Ludden Hall for women and Randall Hall for men, both constructed in 1961, provided much-needed housing for 360 students. Although a wet spring and delays in construction materials postponed occupancy dates until almost the end of the first semester, these two dorms provided innovative features. Partitions between every other room provided built-in storage space that could be removed to make the two rooms into one large room. More importantly, both were air conditioned for use during the summer school sessions. In addition, the rooms no longer included individual lavatories, and students used central restrooms on each floor.

Believing a good sports program was also a good recruiting tool, President Cushing, a former athlete, moved to upgrade Kearney athletics. In 1959 he increased the seating in Foster Field from 2,900 to 4,700 and added a heated press box for sports writers and announcers. Then, after visiting over 30 comparable colleges in South Dakota, Kansas, Missouri, Minnesota, New Mexico, Utah, and Wyoming, he related that "he had not found one college with facilities so handicapping students who need health, physical education, and recreational training as the physical education building at Kearney." He protested that under the present mill levy, it would take 10 years to accumulate enough money to build the proposed gymnasium, so with the approval of the board of trustees, a request was made to the legislature for an appropriation of state funds. Cushing Coliseum became a reality in 1961. Although the cost was a hefty $1.3 million, it accommodated three classrooms; a basketball court seating 3,600; 212 lockers and storage space; a 220-yard indoor dirt track with a broad-jump pit, a pole-vault runway, and a shot-put area; a 75-by-45-by-12-foot swimming pool that featured an underwater observation area as well as underwater lighting; offices for the physical education staff; separate locker room facilities for faculty; and a concession stand. The college used the building for the first time to inaugurate their fifth president, Dr. Hassel.

Cushing Coliseum

Inter-High School Scholastic Contest winners

TRADITIONS ❖ Throughout the KSTC years, seniors sporadically continued the tradition of class gifts. Some included entrance pillars donated by the class of 1925, stage curtains given by the class of 1929, and the life-size statue of Jeanne d'Arc contributed by the 1933 French students.

The college also started new traditions. The first Inter-High School Scholastic Contest was held on campus April 8, 1927, and provided Nebraska students the opportunity to compete in academic fields rather than just in athletics. All schools were eligible to compete for the grand trophy, awarded to schools scoring the most points; schools with fewer than 150 students could also compete for the Master Trophy. In 1928, 9 towns brought 45 students. In 1951 competition grew to 90 towns and 1,417 students. By 1959, 2,055 students from 133 schools participated. When the contest became too large in 1969 with 3,800 students, the college discontinued the program.

Celebrations also marked the KSTC years. In June 1930 the school celebrated its twenty-fifth anniversary, themed "We Mark with Light," highlighted by a reunion with first president A. O. Thomas and several original faculty members. During the 1920s the Alumni Association, incorporated in 1927, had sponsored a drive to purchase a $10,000 Estey organ with 1,000 pipes. They donated it to the music department during the anniversary celebration and dedicated it to Harriet Sutton, a former physical science instructor and past secretary of the Alumni Association who initiated the organ fund. George T. Devereux of the Estey Organ Company played a dedicatory concert on the organ, even though not all of the pipes had been installed. The college also presented a pageant directed by Professor C. T. Ryan at Harmon Park. *The Spirit of Education* reenacted six scenes in the history of the college to an audience of more than 3,000.

The Alumni Association also spearheaded the fiftieth anniversary on June 15, 1955, attended by the wife of first president A. O. Thomas as well as members of the first graduating class of 1906 and again using the theme "We Mark with Light." Doyle Howitt, vice president of the student council, welcomed the guests. In his speech, President Cushing said, "Education is the means man uses to tie the progress of the past into the present for the sake of the future." The alumni presented an historical pageant highlighting the history of the college. Clayton Morey, a 1940 graduate associated with the Minden Christmas pageant, directed the anniversary tribute, and Professor William Lynn lead a fifty-voice mixed choir that marched down the aisles and onto the stage singing "God of Our Fathers" for the finale.

❖ **ACADEMICS**

With the granting of bachelor's degrees at KSTC, student requirements changed, adding more mandatory classes and emphasizing a more diverse and well-rounded education for teachers-to-be, including a stronger background in educational methods. Faculty, too, were held to higher standards. In 1919, 2 faculty held PhDs, 9 held master's degrees, 15 held bachelor's degrees, and 9 were undergraduates. By 1928, 1 held a PhD, but 15 held master's degrees, 23 held bachelor's degrees, and only 4 were undergraduates. The Normal Board set the teaching load at no less than 18 semester hours, typically six courses per semester, with a reduction in salary if the assignment fell below the standard. Later, accreditation agencies forced the college to reduce the heavy teaching loads, especially when graduate work was assigned.

In 1938 the college returned to the semester rather than the quarter system of academic scheduling. The next year severe budget cuts and a recommendation by the North Central Association of Colleges and Secondary Schools necessitated a major reorganization of the college, reducing the number of departments from 17 to 8: biological sciences, education, fine arts, languages, vocational arts, physical sciences, social sciences, and physical education. The college appointed a chairman to each new department. Unfortunately, the elimination of approximately 11 of 52 faculty

100 NOTABLE PEOPLE

Sena Lang

Housemother Sena Lang watched over the residents of Mens Hall from 1955 to 1969. As one of many preceptresses and housemothers employed by the college, she was responsible for regulating the behavior of students, both male and female (the hall was opened to women during the 1 5-66 school year), and en uring that dorm rooms were kept clean and sanitary. In 2004 a number of former Mens Hall residents paid tribute to Lang with a booklet containing some of their fondest memories of her.

Students in science class

◆ **Durfee Larson**

Major Durfee Larson, a social sciences instructor and graduate of the University of Iowa and the University of Nebraska, was the only KSTC faculty member to speak at an open anti-war meeting on the campus in 1936. When World War II began not long after, he was one of only three professors granted a leave for military service. Larson served in Korea and was reported missing in action in the early part of the fighting. He died in a Communist prisoner–of–war camp in 1953.

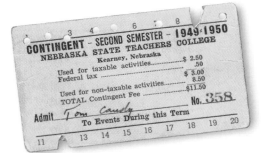

Students typing and keeping books

positions followed the reduction. The largest outcry protested the "indefinite leave of absence" of Anna V. Jennings, one of the original faculty.

During World War II, the college curriculum focused not only on training teachers but preparing men and women to serve their nation, and convocation attendance became compulsory for the duration of the war. Emphasis shifted to courses such as intense typing, shorthand, mathematics, and bookkeeping to fill the need for civil service workers, and students registered increasing numbers for physical education to prepare for serving their nation at war. Faculty enrolled in first aid classes.

By 1942 enrollment was down 25 percent. To bolster the numbers, President Herbert L. Cushing urged students to help the cause by furthering their education: "If you are to play your part in the great drama now being enacted upon the great world stage, you must be prepared. The college at Kearney is streamlining its program in an effort to aid the youth of Nebraska to carry their share of winning the war."

Through special revised programs, college men who wished to continue their education could be eligible for "deferred service," as long as war conditions permitted, by enlisting and continuing college through graduation before being called to active duty. By attending summer school, students could graduate in three years. The college also teamed with the U.S. Army's Air Forces in offering an aviation cadet training program as well as a cooperative program with the Navy that allowed college men to continue through their sophomore year before joining. In addition, college credit would be accepted for approved training programs in the military service.

After World War II many teachers who had stopped teaching to serve in the military or work at better-paying jobs created during wartime did not return to teaching, causing a severe shortage. To alleviate the problem, the state issued temporary certificates that enabled people without proper training in educational methods to teach in the public schools, encouraging more to enter the field. President Cushing responded by calling for higher standards for certification at KSTC to maintain the quality of education and teachers.

With interest growing for non-teaching degrees, 1,375 college students from Kearney, Wayne, Chadron, and Peru signed a petition circulated in 1946-47 to allow the four Nebraska State Teachers Colleges to grant degrees in liberal arts. The legislature allowed KSTC to grant its first non-teaching degree, the bachelor of arts, in 1949. The new liberal arts degree necessitated major changes, so in 1954 the college created a program of basic studies that required all students to take specific general classes to complete their degree, giving them a well-rounded background. Students were now required to take 46 semester hours from four blocks: personal adjustment (9); English, language, and fine arts (17); science (9); and social science (11). Requirements for graduation would also include 32 hours in a major course of study and 21 hours in a minor. The common professional sequence in education required 23 hours for a degree.

Although the end of the war caused class sizes to increase dramatically, financial aid did not keep pace with the growing student body. In 1958 only five scholarships were available for students who had completed one year's work. In 1959 the Kearney State College Endowment Association was incorporated to accept grants and gifts from outside sources to supplement state funds and to match federal loan funds being made available to students.

❖ **COURSE OFFERINGS**

Summer school continued to play an important role in the life of the college by catering to teachers who wanted to upgrade their certificates and schools whose librarians needed to meet the standards set by the North Central Association. Illustrated posters advertised the city, school, and curriculum. By 1929 the school offered two six-week half terms, keeping the training school in session the entire summer so students could complete their practice teaching. During the Depression, the college doubled its efforts to attract students by advertising the affordable cost of education.

In 1921 the college organized an extension department, directed by Ralph Noyer, to keep teachers abreast of their profession and to inform college faculty of actual teaching problems in Nebraska education. Over half of the faculty conducted classes in 27 study centers—from Omaha to Burwell to Danbury. At first the student cost was only the hotel and travel expenses of the teacher, but later the college charged a $3 per credit-hour fee. One hour of credit demanded at least 15 lecture hours or eight written assignments in classes ranging from interior decoration and football coaching to college algebra and business psychology.

GRADUATE WORKSHOPS

SUMMER, 1963

Nebraska State Teachers College
KEARNEY

Joe Lutjeharms

After graduating from KSTC in 1958, Joe Lutjeharms went on to become a teacher and administrator in Kansas, Colorado, and Nebraska. He later became deputy commissioner of education for the Nebraska Department of Education and in 1983 was named Nebraska's commissioner of education. Lutjeharms earned a doctorate from the University of Northern Colorado in 1968 and received an honorary Doctor of Humane Letters from UNK in 1993 for his work as a leader in Nebraska education. The school awarded him a Distinguished Service Award in 1984 and a Distinguished Alumni Award in 1990.

Other changes modified college traditions. The compulsory daily chapel during the Normal School years dwindled to one per week and then two per month until the gatherings were discontinued because the auditorium could no longer hold the total student body. The administration modified the gatherings into optional convocations that featured celebrated musicians, writers, politicians, scientists, and religious leaders, such as William Howard Taft, William Jennings Bryan, **Helen Keller**, John G. Neihardt, Will Durant, Carl Sandburg, Vachel Lindsay, Bishop Gerald Kennedy, President Franklin D. Roosevelt (by radio), **Senator John F. Kennedy**, Nelson Eddy, Jimmy Dorsey, Benny Goodman, Glenn Miller, and *New York Times* reporter and KSTC graduate Bess Furman.

Helen Keller visit   *John F. Kennedy visit*

VOCATIONAL ARTS ◆ Course offerings also changed with the times. Vocational arts expanded greatly during the KSTC years, changing its name from manual arts to industrial education in 1922. Until the construction of the new vocational arts building in 1956, the department had been housed in the south wing basement of the Administration building and the coal room of the old heating plant.

In 1928, in addition to featuring courses in mechanical drawing and home mechanics, vocational education began offering an engineering course in model airplane construction. Advanced woodworking students drafted and constructed 30 teachers' desks, 24 work benches, 12 drawing tables, 24 stools, and 13 dining tables for use on campus.

During World War II the government needed trained welders and draftsmen in the war factories as well as architectural and construction crews to erect barracks and training camp buildings. The Kearney program offered new courses to meet this challenge. By 1950, 73 percent of America's workforce was employed in production or manufacturing jobs to meet the demand for new buildings and projects, so industrial education again changed its focus, planning its curriculum to fit business needs as well as to prepare those who planned to teach industrial arts in the public schools.

Students in a cooking class

Frank Lydic

As one of the first cross country runners at KSTC, Frank Lydic was one of the few to receive recognition outside of Nebraska. In 1929 he won the Midwest AAU Junior one-mile race and set several school and conference records. He finished ninth at a national meet in Chicago in 1929 and placed in the 3000-meter run the following year. In 1931 when the world record for the one-mile was 4:10.4, Lydic ran a 4:17.9. After graduating he reached the finals of the 1932 Olympic trials in the 1500-meter run and the semi–finals of the 1936 Olympic trials in the 5000-meter run. Lydic was elected to the KSC Athletic Hall of Fame in 1980.

Home economics continued to attract women, especially when Romayne Webster, a certified Smith-Hughes Teacher, became department head. The Smith-Hughes National Vocational and Educational Act of 1917 provided federal funds to support the teaching of vocational educational programs by paying the salaries of teachers, supervisors, and directors of home economics, agriculture, trade, and industrial subjects. In 1926 Webster began working diligently to acquire a house on campus, a requirement for the program, where majors would live for a definite time and manage the household duties. The care, nutrition, and management of a baby were also standard at such practice houses. At that time, the only place teachers could secure Smith-Hughes training was at the University of Nebraska. But despite the lack of such a laboratory at Kearney, the department had its largest enrollment in history in 1926 because of the growing demand for high school home economic teachers. The classes in food study doubled in size, and Webster's courses in millinery were as popular as her fashion shows, which purportedly attracted 100 percent of the male students.

Because of the well-established college farm, vital to the campus since its beginning in providing milk, meat, potatoes, and vegetables for the cafeteria, vocational arts was able to offer a Smith-Hughes agricultural course in 1926. However, because of the drought and Depression, the 51-acre farm was leased in 1936, and the equipment sold at auction.

With the completion in 1955 of the Otto C. Olsen Vocational Arts building, the expanded facilities resulted in increased enrollment and the need for additional faculty. The department grew from three to eight faculty members in just one year. Industrial arts now offered work in seven areas: woodworking, power mechanics, machine shop, general metals, crafts, graphic arts, and mechanical drawing. Crafts, popular with all students, included courses in lapidary and the jewelry arts, plastics and leather, and crafts in community life. Driver and general

Homer McConnell

Homer McConnell won the first "popularity contest" at KSTC in 1925. He was voted second most popular the following year. Although an active member of the History Club, Emanon Literary Society, Zip Club, and Pi Kappa Delta, McConnell still managed to find time to serve as chairman of the Student Government Constitution Committee. He took an active role in establishing the school's student government and was elected its first president in 1926. McConnell worked as a principal, superintendent, and the director of the U.S. Food and Drug Administration Training Program after graduation. Later he worked for the U.S. Department of Health, Education, and Welfare. He received an Outstanding Alumni Award in 1985.

College Print Shop

safety education, introduced by Olson in the late 1930s, continued to serve prospective teachers. In addition, the home economics department finally acquired a campus home-management house, furnished by Kearney merchant H. W. Swan from his used furniture business. It functioned as a laboratory for students from 1955 to 1970. A preschool laboratory and child development courses were also added upon the completion of the Olsen building. The college Print Shop, the idea of President Cushing, a former linotype operator, began operating during the fall of 1957 for students in graphic arts, journalism, and industrial education. Eugene Buck taught printing classes, and Thomas Flack, a commercial printer and linotype specialist, took charge of all campus printing jobs, including the publication of the *Antelope*.

BUSINESS AND ❖ FINE ARTS

The business department, also housed in the Olsen building, started out in 1905 with one class in bookkeeping, which became a two-year course of study in 1917, mainly training teachers. By 1938 shorthand, typing, accounting, and business ethics rounded out the program.

Fine Arts, too, flourished at KSTC. Music continued to draw students, especially when the groups began touring. In 1922 the Men's Ensemble (21 voices) enjoyed a two-week singing tour in the Colorado Rockies while the female St. Cecilians (27 voices) spent two days touring surrounding towns and joining in concert with the men in February. A mixed chorus of students and townspeople presented Haydn's *The Creation* in 1927 to an audience of 1,500 in the college auditorium, and in 1929 formed the Central Nebraska Choral Union, 250 voices strong, to perform in the area. In observance of the silver jubilee in 1930, the combined choruses presented Handel's

Messiah. From 1942 to 1947, the choir consisted of women's voices only, since most of the men were at war. In 1942 the annual choir tour was cancelled because of the tire shortage.

The college orchestra, which once consisted of 8 pieces, including the professor, had grown to 40 members by 1927 and boasted of a full symphony orchestra of 60 by 1932, with instruments valued at more than $10,000. The orchestra gave concerts around the state. The war took three years from the life of the group, but it reorganized in 1945. By 1950 the orchestra presented *The Student Prince* with the college male chorus. Elizabeth Harris and Don Welch sang the leads.

Also growing steadily, the college band numbered 23 members by 1925, playing at numerous athletic contests and spring concerts. After a brief decline to six members in 1930, it increased steadily in membership and proficiency. During the 1954 season, the band adopted the West Point style

The college orchestra

The college band

Lyle E. Mantor ◆

Lyle E. Mantor joined KSTC in 1927 as a professor and chairman of the Department of History. He chaired the Division of Social Sciences after the academic reorganization of the institution in 1939. He continued to serve in that capacity until 1961 and continued to teach until 1964. A graduate of the Iowa State Teachers College, Mantor earned his master's and PhD at the University of Iowa, where in 1927, he completed his dissertation on the history of Fort Kearny. The Lyle E. Mantor Residence Hall opened in 1965.

❖ **John Marrow**

John Marrow, a Kearney native, was the first athlete from KSTC to play professional football. An All-Conference tackle and dual-sport letter winner in football (1935, 1936) and track (1936, 1937), Marrow played professional football for the Chicago Cardinals and St. Louis Gunners from 1938 to 1940 and then went on to coach high school and, later, university athletics. He was selected to play in the Professional All-Star game in Chicago in 1937. Marrow was a member of the U.S. Olympic Planning Commission for the 1984 Olympics in Los Angeles, and in 1980 he was elected to the KSC Athletic Hall of Fame.

of uniforms in blue and gold and performed intricate drills at halftime entertainments. One annual activity sponsored by the music department was Band Day, an event featuring a parade and halftime program. Faculty and faculty spouses helped prepare lunch for hundreds of participants from area high schools.

Drama played a central role in campus life as well. Between 1910 and 1955, students performed 90 plays, 8 of them by Shakespeare, directed by 21 different faculty members. When the tradition of the Senior Class play ended in 1936, major productions dropped, and finally, during the years of World War II, the Drama League produced no major plays. In 1948 the group began producing plays again, featuring *Our Hearts Were Young and Gay*. Since that time, except during the years when no stage was available, the college typically produced four major plays a year.

Music and drama students combined their talents for many productions, such as *Desert Song* and *Blossom Time* in the 1930s; *Annie Get Your Gun*, *Brigadoon*, and *Show Boat* in the 1950s; and *South Pacific* and *Music Man* in the early 1960s. However, with the inadequate staging area and structural failure of the auditorium in the Administration building, all major productions had to cease until new facilities were available.

Debate continued in popularity in the 1920s. The Forensic League joined the national fraternity Pi Kappa Delta in 1924, and in 1926 debate became a part of course offerings. However, joining the national organization caused controversy among conference colleges, especially when the debate question selected by Pi Kappa Delta for 1925-26 considered the proposed sale of light beer and wines and, again, in 1954-55 when the debate issue centered on diplomatic relations with the Communist government of China. President Cushing, one of the most vocal objectors to the China debate question, felt it would be "indoctrinating" students with an un-Democratic philosophy.

Debate team

College radio program

In 1930 Kearney won its first state championship in debate. The team traveled to Honolulu University in 1938 to attend the Aloha Tournament. Women, too, began winning intercollegiate competitions, beginning with the team of Addah Jane Ludden and Florence Williams in 1939-40. Between 1940 and 1963, Kearney students placed first 77 times in the Nebraska Intercollegiate Forensic Association Tournament in debate, extemporaneous speaking, oratory, and peace oratory as well as posted victories in regional and national Pi Kappa Delta tournaments.

Broadcasting joined the college in 1931. The first radio program from KSTC (on the first day of broadcasting for the new Kearney station, KGFW-AM) broadcast the Kearney vs. Wesleyan football game on Thanksgiving Day. Campus radio programs originated around 1936 when President Cushing began his tenure. He saw radio as a public relations tool, so he purchased equipment to make it possible to broadcast over KGFW-AM from the campus. Professor Calvin T. Ryan began his Sunday School Lesson of the Air over KGFW-AM in a revamped two-car garage studio behind Green Terrace Hall. By 1938 Ryan's journalism classes were presenting three programs weekly, and students could sign up for Radio in the Classroom through the English department. No other college in Nebraska offered a radio program. The college installed a studio and control room on the second floor of the north wing of the Administration building in 1940. And in 1946 the campus began broadcasting daily programs from KGFW-AM's 250-watt station.

When KGFW-AM management changed hands, it required the campus station to purchase air time. The college obtained permission in 1956 from the Federal Communications Commission to operate its own station, KOVF-FM, "The Voice of the Friendly College." Fully licensed by the FCC and operating at 550 kilocycles, the station broadcast to all buildings on campus from 3 to 5 p.m. KOVF-FM switched to Kearney's newest radio station, the 5,000-watt KRNY-FM, and started

100 Notable People

George E. Martin

George E. Martin, a graduate of the University of Nebraska, was elected in 1919 as the third president of KSTC. Martin arrived at the Normal School in 1915 as head of the English department. He was appointed dean of teacher training in 1917. During the 17 years he served as president, the school's two-year degree program was extended to four years, and the institution became a fully accredited teachers college. In 1935 he was selected president of the National Education Association. He died the following year.

broadcasting through the new station's transmitter, extending its hours from 5 p.m. to 11 p.m. Lucky Strike Cigarette Corporation sponsored the newscasts and made it possible for the station to have 24-hour international teletype service from United Press International. In August 1961 the college remodeled the studio and purchased new equipment. Stan Miller, a sophomore with seven years' experience in radio and television, managed the station and implemented many of the changes. The goal of the station was not only to entertain but to train students in operating broadcast media, creating advertising, and writing programs.

DEPARTMENT OF ❖
EDUCATION

A.O. Thomas Laboratory School

The Department of Education weathered a series of economic ups and downs during the KSTC years. After 1926 the A. O. Thomas Laboratory School served the K-12 system, offering programs in college preparatory, industrial education, home economics, and commerce, and many students practiced teaching there. By 1935, 110 students were enrolled, but a lack of funding forced the closure of the high school in 1938-39. As a result, secondary student teachers observed in Kearney schools until 1954 when the education department instigated an off-campus program for secondary student teachers with cooperating public schools. The school discontinued teaching seventh and eighth grades in 1940 because of low enrollment. As pupil numbers continued to decline, elementary grades were combined until eventually President Cushing required that the children of faculty members attend the school. After Wayne Marshall became the director of the Thomas School in 1956, enrollment increased dramatically. When the Normal Board finally ordered the school's closing in 1963, seven full-time teachers were teaching packed classrooms. Budget woes coupled with the inadequacy of one school to handle the profusion of student teachers needing placement influenced the decision.

Despite the changes, the teacher training program remained strong and was one of the first 200 institutions to be certified by the National Council for the Accreditation of Teacher Education (NCATE) when it was established in 1954.

COLLEGE EXPENSES ❖

As the academic offerings increased after the Normal School became a State Teachers College, many of the students' expenses increased as well. In 1922 room rent ranged from 50¢ to $1 a week, and meals cost 18¹⁄₂¢ each. Textbook rental added $10. Tuition was not charged until 1939 at 50¢ a credit hour.

By 1947, along with a reduced college catalogue due to the paper shortage, room and board cost $2 a week for a double room (plus 50¢ if students brought a radio). Tuition was later amended to a $60 flat fee per semester, but it did not cover the cost of instruction, which was still paid for by the state in 1955. The fee covered special programs, athletic events, the *Antelope*, and "fringe benefits." By 1955 semester rates for rooms had risen to $54, meals to $150, but the flat fee remained at $60; one semester of college cost students on the average $274. However, KSTC now offered 20 major fields of study and 5 degrees: a bachelor of arts in education, a bachelor of fine arts in education, a bachelor of science in education, a bachelor of music in education, and a bachelor of arts. The matriculation fee in 1905 was $5 good for life. Fifty years later, it was still $5.

One of the fringe benefits included Student Health Services, created in 1921 to meet the demands of the increased student enrollment following World War I. Lillian Stuff, RN, served as the first nurse in the office in the Administration building. Health care on campus was especially critical during the influenza epidemic of the 1920s. With the hiring of Eleanor Stromquist, RN, in 1928, a program in School Health Education offered courses such as Health Education in Elementary Schools, The Teacher's Health, as well as home nursing and first aid. During the Depression years of 1933 to 1938, the college suspended student health services and in 1938 moved student health to the auxiliary gym (Copeland) and hired Alta Bergquist, RN, BA, to care for students' need—from minor scrapes to the life-threatening polio epidemic of the 1940s and 1950s. In 1959 the college contracted with Kearney Clinic to have a physician on campus. Bergquist remained in her position 28 years until her retirement in 1966.

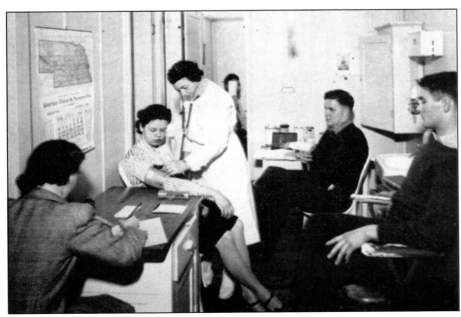

Student Health Services

◆ Clayton Morey

Clayton Morey, a 1940 graduate of KSTC, helped found
the Kearney State College
Foundation in 1959. As one
of eight founding members,
he served on the foundation
board for 23 years and acted
as president for 2 years.
In 1946 with Reverend Art
Johnson, he co-authored the
Minden Christmas pageant
"The Light of the World,"
which is still produced each
December. He entered the
insurance business in Minden
in 1944 and directed and
produced more than 50
plays in the Minden area
throughout his career. KSTC
awarded him a Distinguished
Alumni Award in 1982.

STUDENT LIFE ❖

The four decades of the KSTC years saw student life go from the Roaring
Twenties to the Depression and the Dirty Thirties, the wartime forties, and
the conservative fifties. The drastic changes America experienced reverberat-
ed on the Kearney campus.

As society's standards became more relaxed in the 1920s, extracurricular
activities flourished. A "Shirt Tail Parade" held on Central Avenue on July
25, 1925, exemplified this social atmosphere. The *Kearney Daily Hub*
reported that the male students who had been attending summer session
and living in "Tent City" celebrated the end of classes by marching down
25th Street and then south down Central Avenue in their night shirts,
stopping in open businesses and giving the college yell, and finally staging
a ghost dance on the corner of Central and 23rd Street. "They broke the
quiet but nothing else."

Although wearing nightshirts in public did not become common practice
during the KSTC years, mass production made clothing more affordable, and
styles became colorful, less formal, and, with the abandonment of the corset,
more comfortable. The 1920s ushered in the Flapper Age when hemlines
grew alarmingly short, waistlines disappeared, and women dared to bob
their hair, shorten their sleeves, and bare part of their arms. However, during
the 1930s, clothing became a luxury. When sleeveless dresses became fashionable, many of the young women, who wanted to be in style but could
not afford new clothing, cut off the sleeves of their dresses. Dean of Women
Ruth Elliott convened the immodest offenders and ordered them
to sew the sleeves back on their dresses. During the 1940s, skirts modestly
lengthened, much to the chagrin of campus men. However, sweaters
retained their popularity, and in 1949 the campus featured a Sweater Day,
culminating with a Sweater Dance and the choosing of a Sweater Queen.

Honor Convocation
and
Senior Recognition Day

May 7, 1946

K

NEBRASKA STATE TEACHERS COLLEGE
KEARNEY, NEBRASKA

Loper spirit on display 1956

Students enjoying some free time

Mary L. Morse ◆

Mary L. Morse, known affectionately by many of her students as "Dr. Mary," had been a member of the faculty for nearly 20 years when she died suddenly of a heart attack in 1958. She joined the KSTC staff in 1937, but from 1942 to 1945 taught at the Mississippi College for Women. She returned to Kearney as a professor of chemistry because she missed the mid-western attitudes, climate, and friendliness. Born in 1896 in St. Louis, Missouri, Morse received her BS in 1919 and her master's in 1920 from the University of Michigan. She earned her PhD from the University of Minnesota in 1929. One of the lecture halls attached to Bruner Hall of Science is named in her honor.

A dress code persisted through the 1950s and into the 1960s. Women could wear only a shirtwaist dress or skirt with a blouse or sweater and flats or loafers to class and to the library. Sunday noon and Wednesday evening demanded dress clothes, but after 4:30 p.m. and on weekends, casual clothes, Bermudas or slacks, were permitted. In their rooms, women could relax in shorts, jeans, and "grubbies," but such apparel was not permitted in the lounge in the evenings or on Sunday afternoons. No such code existed for the men.

The College Women's League, formed in 1921 and made up of student representatives and the dean of women, also prescribed behavior expectations. The league published handbooks and held convocations regularly to discuss attitudes, rules of conduct, health, vocations, and avocations for young women.

The 1938 handbook *College Girl and Her Personality* outlined the following as acceptable courtesies: "Make introductions correctly; let gentleman walk on the curbside; never take a gentleman's arm during the day; do not eat or chew gum on the street; always wear a hat to church, the theater, a restaurant, and concerts; avoid vulgarity in dress. In class, do not chew gum or put your feet on the desk in front of you; avoid private conversations in class; don't be late; don't monopolize class discussion; open doors for older women; do not litter. At the table, keep your feet on the floor and your elbows off of the table; dip soup spoons away from you and sip from the side; break bread and rolls in small portions and butter each separately."

The 1938 clothing and textiles class also prepared a booklet titled *Looking Smart on Campus* that not only explained how to dress for college in the current styles, but also described what kind, what color, and how many types of clothing to bring to campus, including five to six sets of underwear "in good, usable condition" and two to three dozen handkerchiefs.

Adolph "Pat" Panek

Adolph "Pat" Panek was a nine-time letter winner in football, basketball, and track at KSTC between 1922 and 1925. After graduation he coached high school football at three different Nebraska schools before moving to Colorado in 1938. He continued coaching in Denver until 1977. Over the course of 52 seasons, Panek accumulated 328 wins, which was second highest in the nation at the time of his retirement. Panek has been inducted into the Colorado Sports Hall of Fame (1976), the UNK Athletic Hall of Fame (1980), the Colorado High School Activities Association Hall of Fame (1991), the National Federation of State High School Associations' National High School Hall of Fame (1995), and the Nebraska High School Sports Hall of Fame (2004).

STUDENT ❖
ORGANIZTIONS

Students at a dance at Fort Kearney ballroom 1955

Students at a dance in Cushing Coliseum 1963

The college encouraged socializing, especially in supervised clubs and organizations. When the administration finally permitted dancing on campus, "sundown" or hour dances in the gymnasium were popular. For special occasions, students held parties in the Crystal Room of the Fort Kearney Hotel or danced at the pavilion on Kearney Lake. However, authorities prohibited smoking and alcoholic beverages on campus, although punch was occasionally spiked, and they restricted students from attending dances at the 1733 Ballroom west of the city limits. The dean required women to have permission from their parents to date men from the Army air base east of Kearney.

Sigma Tau Delta English honorary

Calvin T. Ryan ◆

Calvin T. Ryan arrived at KSTC in 1928 and quickly accepted the dual roles of head of the English department and chairman of the Division of Language and Literature. In the classroom he experimented with the use of radio, and through his own interest and with the assistance of a local radio station, he helped to establish a radio broadcasting program at the school in the early 1930s. He was awarded an honorary doctorate in 1963 from Iowa Wesleyan University, where he taught before coming to Nebraska. Ryan retired in 1958. The new KSC library was dedicated the Calvin T. Ryan Library that same year.

Clubs rounded out life at KSTC, and students began gaining recognition in honor societies, speech contests, and student government. Many focused in academic areas such as Band Club, Science Club, and foreign language clubs that complemented coursework. The English Reformers organized in 1926, and they formulated the Ten Commandments of English to make "good English a habit." Honor societies, like Xi Phi (academics), Phi Beta Kappa (forensics), Pi Kappa Delta (debate), Sigma Tau Delta (English), Pi Omega Pi (business), Lambda Delta Lambda (science), and Phi Gamma Mu (social science) quickly formed. In 1926 the Student National Education Association formed; it was the first one to be founded in the United States. Students also organized a formal government, adopted a constitution, and elected Homer McConnell as the first Student Council president.

The YWCA, YMCA, and Catholic Club became increasingly active in service projects and provided religious organizations for the students after required daily chapel services were discontinued. Other denominational organizations appeared throughout these years as well, such as the Lutheran Club organized in 1940, and the Intervarsity Christian Fellowship, established after World War II, which concentrated on interdenominational Bible study.

Fraternities and sororities had little support in the early years. In 1922 President Martin considered the Greek social organizations as "problems," and the college did not officially recognize any of them, so few records exist about them in the campus newspaper or yearbooks. However, by 1935 half of the students attending KSTC were members of a fraternity or sorority. Even as late as 1954, rumors spread that the fraternities and sororities would be prohibited on campus, but President Cushing only urged that changes be made within these organizations to bring them in line with campus policies.

❖ **Edith M. Smithey**

As a student at the Normal School, Edith M. Smithey worked part-time in the registrar's office. She accepted a full-time position following her graduation in 1915. In 1919 she was made an assistant registrar, and in 1923 she accepted the role of registrar. For the next three decades, as the final authority on all students' grades, she had a reputation for adhering to graduation requirements so rigidly that she inspired the phrase: "The Lord willing and Miss Smithey permitting, you will graduate." Although Smithey resigned in 1955, she was considered so essential to the interpretation of early records that she agreed to work as an assistant registrar at the school for four more years.

Delta Phi Beta members 1954

To establish credibility, a movement began in the 1960s for the Greeks to take a stronger role in campus life and to affiliate with national organizations. The first sorority, the Juanita Girls, organized in 1910, became Delta Phi Beta in 1944, and then in 1962 joined the national sorority Chi Omega. Several other sororities followed suit about this same time: Sigma Theta Phi, founded in 1915, became Gamma Phi Beta in 1963, the only sorority with off-campus housing on 615 West 26th. Zeta Chi Alpha, organized in 1935, affiliated with the national Alpha Xi Delta in 1962, and Kappa Alpha Phi, founded in 1956, became Alpha Phi in 1963. That year, with the organization of Delta Zeta, five nationally affiliated sororities actively rushed for new pledges at KSTC.

Few fraternities joined national associations during the KSTC years, for they concentrated on establishing residency houses off-campus. The oldest fraternity, Phi Tau Gamma, founded in 1915, became the first group in the 1930s to have a fraternity house on West 25th Street; by 1960 they had moved to 2221 7th Avenue. The Caledonians, the second to organize in 1916, became Sigma Phi Epsilon in 1963 with a fraternity house at 2304 6th Avenue.

In addition, several new fraternities organized on campus. Phi Phi Phi (Tri Phi), founded in 1955, established a house at 521 West 25th and had a Saint Bernard mascot, Ambrose, who lived in the house and was nominated for student body president in 1969. The next year, Omega Delta Pi and Sigma Upsilon Nu (which became Theta Xi from 1962 to 2002) organized. In 1961 Kappa Lambda Chi was founded, establishing a house at 611 25th Street. In 1962 they also affiliated with a national house, Sigma Tau Gamma.

Less formal clubs also added color to college life. Some organized for light-hearted fun, like the Order of Pink-Haired Sheiks and Shebas for redheads only. The Boars International included prominent male athletes residing at the Midway Hotel. Established in 1935, the club boasted of holding all-night "bull sessions" and an annual spring outing that lasted several days. The men also managed the election of the gridiron queen and held a "spring frolic" after track season. Despite their seeming lack of academic display, they also boasted a higher scholastic average than any of the fraternities or sororities.

❖ WORLD WAR II

Just as World War I had affected the Kearney campus, so did the entrance of the United States into World War II, and many KSTC men and women began to enlist. On December 23, 1940, 45 men of Kearney Company D mobilized; they were joined by another 33 and became a part of a division of 25,000 soldiers. After 13 weeks of intensive training, they were assigned to transport fuel, food, and forage for the division. Many of the students rose to the ranks of corporal, sergeant, and staff sergeant and transferred to other companies.

Support surged among faculty and students on campus. The 1943 *Blue and Gold* especially reflected this liaison. The yearbook's cover replicated khaki green material, and freshman became known as Privates, financial aid personnel were designated Paymasters, and President Cushing was named Commander-in-Chief. The Women's League also supported the war, telling the young women, "The Nation is at war and when you arrive you will see many service men from the nearby airfield from every state in the country. Through U.S.O. work every girl who has reached the age of eighteen or is a high school graduate has the opportunity to help entertain these boys at weekly dances and hours spent at the U.S.O. Several girls serve at the Red Cross Canteen and do their little share in making the boys happy through food and cheery smiles. . . . Do as you will, but remember your school."

Lt. Donald W. Johnson, who enlisted in 1939 before America had declared war, was the college's first death in 1942. National Guard companies, who left for further training in 1940, were the initial contingents called up. Larry Gardner, former Kearney student, served under Gen. Douglas MacArthur's bomber command in the Phillipines. The United States awarded him the Silver Star for gallantry. The 1946 *Blue and Gold* lists each of the men and how they died. Returning veterans, because of their special bond formed through common wartime experiences, formed the Veterans Club on campus.

H.G. Stout

H. G. Stout joined the KSTC staff first as a professor of education and then as chairman of the Division of Education in 1939. In 1951 he was appointed the school's first dean of instruction, and in the months following President George S. Martin's death, Stout chaired a three-member faculty committee to administer the college's affairs. In 1963 West Hall was renamed H. G. Stout Hall in his honor.

Members of the Veterans Club

Bernhard F. Stutheit

Bernard F. Stutheit, a graduate of the University of Nebraska, joined KSTC in 1943 after serving as the superintendent of Nebraska public schools. He was appointed dean of men in 1945 and dean of students in 1954. When he retired in 1973, a lounge in the Memorial Student Union (now Student Affairs Building) was officially dedicated the Bernard F. Stutheit Lounge at the suggestion of students. Stutheit also served the school as a professor of German and speech.

SPORTS ❖ Athletes competed in three different conferences during the KSTC era: the Nebraska Collegiate Conference (NCC) from 1922 to 1930, the Nebraska Intercollegiate Athletic Association (NIAA) from 1930 to 1943, and the Nebraska College Conference (NCC) from 1945 to 1979. In 1922 Fred Fulmer joined the faculty to become the athletic director, and in the beginning, coach of all men's sports. He coached football for 8 seasons and basketball for 10; he also reinstated track, and for a couple of seasons he coached gymnastics. He is credited with sponsoring the first KSC high school track meet in 1929. Beginning in the 1940s, the majority of the competition was at the National Intercollegiate Athletic Association (NIAA) I level. The Antelopes continued the rich tradition begun during the Normal School years, progressing from playing high schools to competing on a national level. Since 1905 two men earned 12 athletic letters: Doyle Fyfe 1951-55 and Gene Armstrong 1954-58. The champion letter winner was Earl Tool who won 16 between 1907 and 1913. However, as the athletic programs became more competitive, eligibility requirements more strict, and more athletes began to specialize in one sport, a letter in each sport became a rarity.

As the sports program grew, the need for new athletic arenas increased. During the 1930-31 school year, the Antelopes finally secured an excellent athletic field west of the gymnasium and on the southwest corner of the intersection of 26th Street and 11th Avenue, constructed to run north-south to avoid facing the sun. Its stands accommodated about 2,000 spectators, bluegrass turf blanketed the field, a board fence surrounded the stadium, and a new system of floodlights, the first in the city, illuminated the night, allowing the Antelopes to play the first college night game west of the Mississippi River. By track season in the spring, a new, cindered quarter-mile runway circled the field. In 1939 Foster Field was completed.

Fred Fulmer and the 1922 football team

❖ **FOOTBALL**

1935 football against Chadron

Merle Trail

Merle Trail was the first
KSTC athlete to receive
All-American recognition.
A four-time letter winner in
football, Trail was selected
NIAA All-Conference tackle
three times between 1928
and 1931 and was voted to
the All-American College
Eleven in 1930. Prevented by
injury from playing much of
the 1931 season (of which
he was elected team
captain), Trail failed to
receive a fourth-straight
all-conference selection.
He was inducted into
the UNK Athletic Hall of
Fame in 1980.

The 1940s provided some of the best teams in the early history of KSTC. Coached by L. F. "Pop" Klein, the 1941 team was undefeated and won the NIAA conference championship, and the 1942 team, finishing 6-2, was declared the "mythical champions." Due to World War II the Kearney squad played no varsity games in 1943 and 1944, but in 1946 when it reorganized, 100 men reported for practice. When the Antelopes began the post-war era, Charlie Foster took the reins as coach from 1945 to 1952, earning a record of 129-132-24.

Marvin "Preacher" Franklin coached in 1953 and 1954 until the arrival of Allen Zikmund, a native of Ord and an All-American end who had played for the University of Nebraska and scored the second touchdown for the Cornhuskers in the 1941 Rose Bowl. After serving in the war, Zikmund returned to Nebraska, coaching high school teams in Alliance and Grand Island before accepting the position in Kearney in 1955. That same year KSTC won the NCC championship in football and played Northern Teachers of Aberdeen, South Dakota, in the Botany Bowl, winning 34-13. Coach Zikmund was named Nebraska College Coach of the Year after the victory and again in 1958 when the team went undefeated and was ranked fifth nationally in the NAIA. Zikmund's teams won NCC championships in 11 of the 17 years he coached.

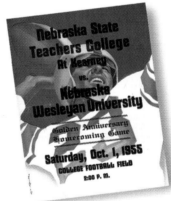

❖ **BASKETBALL AND BASEBALL**

Basketball emerged from a streak of losing seasons in 1922, and except for 1925, continued winning until 1936. Coached by Fred Fulmer, the basketball team won their first NIAA championship in 1923. Fulmer's 1928 and 1929 teams also earned NCC championships, a first for the team. The 1929-30 basketball team, coached by former university star Theodore L. James, was exceptional, traveling over 5,000 miles to play the University of Colorado,

Championships

1928: NIAA Men's Basketball, Men's Cross Country

1929: NIAA Men's Basketball, Men's Cross Country

1930: NIAA Football

1934: NIAA Men's Track

1936: NIAA Football

1937: NIAA Men's Basketball (tie)

1941: NIAA Football, Men's Golf, Men's Tennis, Men's Track

1942: NIAA Men's Golf, Men's Track

1943: NIAA Men's Basketball, Men's Track

1948: NCC Men's Track

1948: NCC Men's Track

1950: NCC Golf, Men's Track

1952: NCC Men's Tennis

1954: NCC Men's Track

1955: NCC Football, Men's Track

1956: NCC Men's Cross Country, Football, Men's Track

1957: NCC Men's Cross Country, Men's Track

1958: NCC Men's Cross Country, Football (tie), Men's Track

1959: NCC Men's Cross Country, Football, Men's Tennis, Men's Track

1960: NCC Men's Cross Country, Men's Track

1961: NCC Men's Cross Country, Men's Tennis, Men's Track

1962: NCC Men's Cross Country, Football, Men's Tennis, Men's Track

1928 men's basketball team (Conference Champs)

1961 baseball

1954 men's golf team

Basketball program

1938 boxing

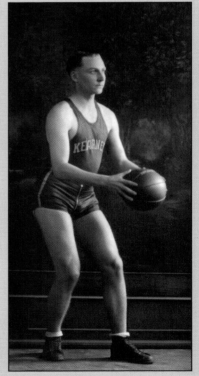

1929 basketball

1954 tennis team

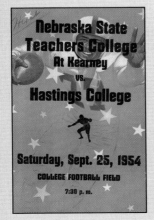

Football program

1955 track team

1930 men's cross country (state and conference champs)

1936 football team (NIAA Champs)

1954 men's basketball

Mary Elaine (Wallace) House

Mary Elaine (Wallace) House, the first woman president of the National Opera Association, graduated from KSTC in 1940; she later received a master's from the University of Illinois. For more than 25 years, she taught voice and directed operas at colleges and universities throughout the country, including Louisiana Tech, New York State University, and Southern Illinois University. Her student production of Britten's *A Midsummer Night's Dream* received favorable reviews among critics in New York. Her written works include *Opera Scenes for Class and Stage* (1979), *More Opera Scenes for Class and Stage: From One Hundred Selected Operas* (1990), and *Upstage, Downstage: A Handbook for Educational Opera Directors* (1992).

Arizona State, Northern Arizona, and New Mexico State and ending the season with a 16-4 record. They also played the Chicago Bears professional team. The Lopers didn't take another NIAA title until 1942. Play moved from the dirt court of "the barn" to the gymnasium following World War I, but since the floor did not meet standard size regulations, the team had to play in neighboring high school gyms. When Kearney High completed their new facility in 1960, KSTC teams could finally play conference games locally, but they did not have their own regulation court until Cushing Coliseum was completed for the 1961-62 season.

Baseball, the most successful of all sports in the Normal School years, was suspended in 1916 and not reinstated until 1961. The team used Kearney's Memorial Field, a WPA project of the Depression years located several blocks northeast of the campus. Coached by Bill Giles from 1961 to 1964, 70 men tried out for the 25-man squad and played a 3-5 season their first year, compiling a 32-26 four-year record.

1961 Baseball team

TRACK AND ❖ CROSS COUNTRY

Coach Fulmer revived competitive track in 1922 for men, suspended during World War I, and won one to three meets a year. Individual track athletes began to gain recognition even before the team started to regularly win conference championships. In the 1940s Merlin Quillen and Robert Hauver excelled in the sprints while Tom Nye dominated the high jump. The track team won NIAA titles from 1937 to 1939 and from 1941 to 1943. Charlie Foster also coached track, and after one year, his team won the championship of the newly formed Nebraska College Conference. His teams continued winning first place trophies from 1947 through 1949.

Track athletes continued to excel throughout the 1950s. In 1952 Glenn Peterson won the NCC 120-yard high hurdles four years in a row. The Lopers had athletes in every NAIA track and field championship from 1955 to 1990, with Clayton Scott winning the NAIA national championship in the two mile in 1955 and 1956 (9:36.3 and 9:28.4). The 1959 team ranked fifth in

1960 KSTC track team competing on Foster Field

the NAIA, and the 1960 team earned sixth. Merlin Lawrence reigned as outdoor NAIA national champion in the pole vault in 1961. During his tenure Coach Foster expanded the KSTC Invitational Track Meet from 28 teams and 200 athletes in 1945 to 120 teams and 1,600 athletes in 1955. In addition to practicing and competing, the coaches and the athletes contributed to building and maintaining the track facilities.

The cross country program, also coached by Fulmer, joined the sports offerings in 1928, and the team won the NIAA championship their first year. Three men comprised the 3-0 cross country team: Frank Lydic, Orlie Watts, and Stewart Hanley. In 1929 they won the Midwestern AAU championship. However, the 1932 season would be their last, for they were the only team in the conference. Occasionally cross country exhibition races were held at football games in the intervening years until Foster renewed cross country in 1956. The team captured conference and district championships from 1957 to 1960, placing second at the national meet in Omaha in 1959.

Herbert Welte

Herbert Welte, a 1924 graduate of KSTC who earned his doctorate from the University of Iowa, became the youngest college president in the United States when he was appointed to that position at the New Britain School in Connecticut in 1929. He then led that institution from a two-year normal school at the time of his appointment to a teacher's college in 1933 and a state college in 1959. Meanwhile, the campus expanded from 2 buildings to 20, and the student population grew from 286 female students to a coeducational institution of over 9,000 students at the time of Welte's retirement in 1968. Welte also helped to establish and develop Central Connecticut State University's athletic program. In 1986 he was awarded a Distinguished Alumni Award from KSC.

❖ **OTHER SPORTS**

KSTC athletes also competed in tennis, golf, boxing, and swimming as intercollegiate sports in the 1930s, but kept few records. When Coach L. F. Klein began coaching tennis in 1931, the squad won NIAA titles for the next six years, playing Hastings, Nebraska Wesleyan, and Fort Hays, among others, for the championship. Discontinued during the war, Marge Elliott re-established the tennis team in 1947, followed by William Morris in 1950, and Les

◆ Rae O. Weimer

Rae O. Weimer left KSTC as a student in 1926 to pursue a career in journalism. After a successful career that included work as a managing editor at New York's experimental *PM* newspaper, Weimer arrived at the University of Florida in 1949. There, he founded and directed the university's College of Journalism and Communication and served as its first dean until his retirement nearly 20 years later in 1968. In 1974 the University of Florida awarded him an honorary Doctor of Letters, and in 1981 the school's new $6.3 million journalism building was named Weimer Hall in his honor.

Women's swimming

Livingston Sr. in 1957. During this time, the tennis and golf teams traveled to competitions with the track teams. In the NCC the tennis teams placed fourth in 1952 and 1954, second in 1956, and first in 1959.

Prior to World War II, under the coaching of Klein, Antelope golfers won three state titles. When golf resumed after the war in 1946, Foster, Morris, and Livingston took over coaching respectively, and the golf team was conference champion or runner-up in 6 of the next 10 years. After that, unfortunately, the team endured a slump until the 1960s.

Women's intercollegiate competition, strong during the Normal School years, basically dropped from the athletic program until the late 1960s. However, the physical education program remained vigorous, with women gaining an athletic field of their own in 1928. In the beginning, "physical training" for women students in the physical education program consisted mostly of folk dancing and gymnastics, which averaged 200 women each quarter. Usually 75 to 100 girls enrolled in swimming each quarter.

Enthusiasm renewed in 1937 with the founding of the Women's Athletic Association, which offered an intramural program in sports, including volleyball, basketball, softball, badminton, and tennis and hosted high school meets in these sports as well. The Naiads synchronized swimming team formed in 1945 and met every week to improve their swimming and diving abilities. The team welcomed men in 1954 and sponsored swim meets and pageants until they disbanded in 1959.

SCHOOL SPIRIT ❖   Sports involved many non-athletes as well. The college pep club, called the Zip Club or Zippers, founded and organized by Carrie Ludden in 1924, chose the cheerleaders, held pep rallies, sold season tickets to athletic events, taught school songs and cheers to the students, and sponsored

K Club

Loper mascot

fund-raising dances and events to purchase white K sweaters for the lettermen. Limited to 40 men and women members, the group lasted until 1955. The K Club formed under the leadership of Coach Ted James in 1930 to support the Zippers and gain added recognition for the lettermen. They also sponsored the annual K Club dance, elected an Athletic King and Queen, sold college pennants, and helped with Homecoming and spring high school track meets.

One of the biggest and longest-running athletic rivalries occurred with the Hastings College Broncos, and during the 1950s and 1960s, students celebrated Bronco Days. The men cut the letter K into their hair or beards, everyone dressed in frontier clothing, each dorm planned special activities, and the campus celebrated with races, snake dances, bonfires, and hangings of broncos in effigy at pep rallies. Harmless at first, the tradition grew out of hand when panty raids in dorms caused damage to buildings and when collegians from each campus committed serious acts of vandalism. Kearney students once destroyed a bell on the Hastings campus, and revengeful Hastings students burned a big H on the Kearney football field. Escalating destruction and inequalities in college populations caused the schools to discontinue competition against one another in 1968.

Other athletic traditions proved more constructive and helped to promote the college across the state. President Cushing, impressed by the Texas Rangerettes precision drill team, encouraged the college in 1955 to create the Wagoneers, who replaced the Zip Club and represented the college at parades and performed at athletic events until 1978.

❖ **CONCLUSION**

Reflecting on the expansion of the college in 1960, President Cushing commented, "We have not only witnessed the dawn of a new decade of the 20th century, but we have witnessed the dawn of a new period of growth on the KSTC campus." The steady, progressive development of the Nebraska State Teachers College at Kearney since its inception as a Normal School reflected the importance of the teachers college in the education of Nebraska children, in the intellectual, social, and cultural development of the students, and in the life of the community. The next 28 years as Kearney State College would prove just as eventful.

KEARNEY
STATE COLLEGE

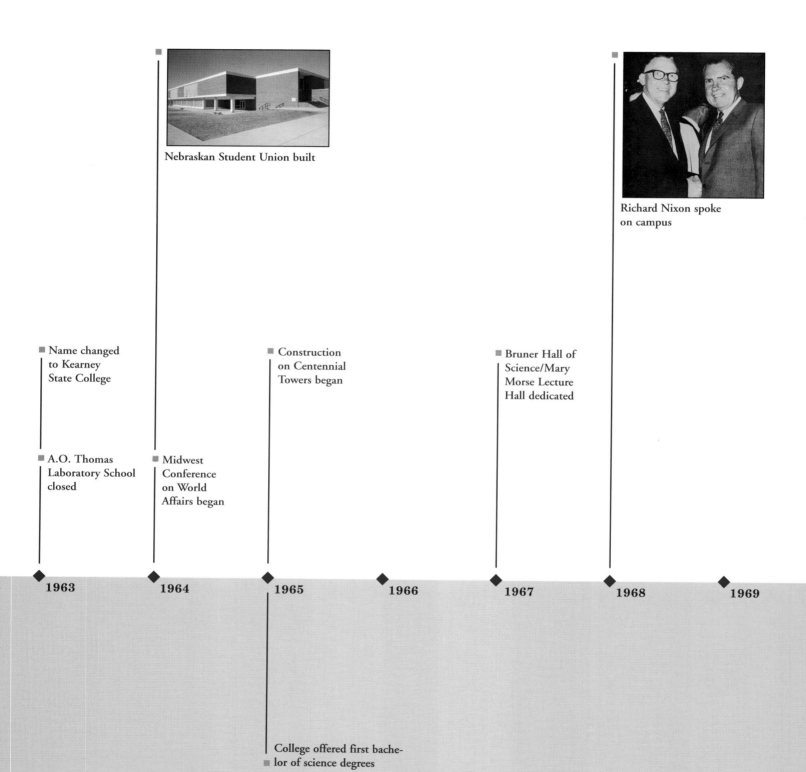

Nebraskan Student Union built

Richard Nixon spoke
on campus

■ Name changed
to Kearney
State College

■ Construction
on Centennial
Towers began

■ Bruner Hall of
Science/Mary
Morse Lecture
Hall dedicated

■ A.O. Thomas
Laboratory School
closed

■ Midwest
Conference
on World
Affairs began

1963   **1964**   **1965**   **1966**   **1967**   **1968**   **1969**

College offered first bache-
■ lor of science degrees

KEARNEY
STATE COLLEGE

Fine Arts building completed

George W. Frank House listed as a
National Historic Site

Platte Valley Review
began publication

Learning Center
created

1970　**1971**　**1972**　**1973**　**1974**　**1975**　**1976**

Bachelor of fine arts
degree approved

Brendan J. McDonald
became president

KEARNEY
STATE COLLEGE

Founders Hall completed

Alumni House listed as a Natonal
Historic Site

Department of
Nursing moved
to West Center

First Career Fair

Campus celebrated its
75th anniversary

| 1977 | 1978 | 1979 | 1980 | 1981 | 1982 | 1983 |

Two-year honors
program created

International
student exchange
program began

William R. Nest
became presiden

KEARNEY
STATE COLLEGE

Old Administration building
demolished

Memorial Carillon Bell
Tower dedicated

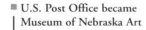 U.S. Post Office became
Museum of Nebraska Art

 Health &
Sports Center
dedicated

Computer terminals
speeded up registration
process

1984	1985	1986	1987	1988	1989	1990

Honors program
expanded to a
four-year program

Department of
Criminal Justice formed

CHAPTER THREE
❖ 1963-1991

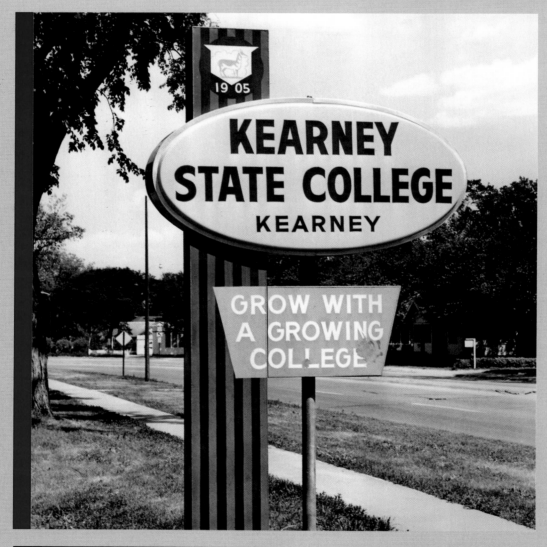

❖ In 1963 the state recognized that Kearney as well as the other three state teachers colleges had become more than teacher education institutions and changed
the names to reflect their individuality and their larger missions. Thus, Kearney
State College, Chadron State College, Wayne State College, and Peru State
College became fully accredited and began offering Nebraska students more
choices than ever.

KEARNEY STATE COLLEGE

❖ **A BROADER MISSION**

|C| ameras flashed as freshman Joyce Iverson of Bridgeport registered for her fall 1961 classes. This milestone signaled the first time that one semester's enrollment had exceeded 2,000, and it forecast the college's future growth. Enrollments would continue to climb as the baby boomer generation reached college age.

The influx of students, however, caused increasing problems for Nebraska State Teachers College at Kearney, and new president Milton J. Hassel faced many challenges. After a 1961 report from the North Central and NCATE accreditation committees indicated that the college ran "a loose ship," the campus went to work to address issues raised in their analysis: rapid enrollment growth without adequate financing, an underfunded graduate program, an informal system of tenure and promotion, heavy teaching loads, and inadequate library facilities and holdings.

What once had been a single-purpose college geared toward preparing future teachers had mushroomed into a multipurpose institution that needed improvement. In 1963 the state recognized that Kearney as well as the other three state teachers colleges had become more than teacher education institutions and changed the names to reflect their individuality and their larger missions. Thus, Kearney State College, Chadron State College, Wayne State College, and Peru State College became fully accredited and began offering Nebraska students more choices than ever.

As enrollments continued to climb in the 1960s, lack of classroom space not only forced academic departments to move into the dormitories, but nationwide teacher shortages also made recruiting new faculty with advanced degrees difficult. However, in 1964 with an increase in enrollment to 3,037 students, KSC was able to hire 29 additional faculty members—9 more than the complete 1905 faculty. The next year, enrollment increased to 3,790, and the college added 49 faculty. By 1966 student numbers had risen to 4,399, and faculty ranks had expanded to 213. President Hassel requested that KSC be permitted to limit enrollment to 5,000 for fall 1968 until adequate facilities could be provided, but the state board would not allow it. In 1970 student numbers reached 5,870, and 35 new hires raised the faculty total to 274.

As the ranks of new teachers swelled, Hal Blostein, political science, and James E. Smith, history, believed that KSC needed a Faculty Senate. Organized in 1970, it became the official voice of the faculty

◆ Donald Briggs

One of the first students to earn a graduate degree from UNK (1957), Donald Briggs joined the faculty immediately after graduation as an instructor in English and journalism. From 1961 to 1974 he served as the school's entire public relations staff and was appointed sports information director in 1974. The Donald K. Briggs Collection in the library houses 64,000 items, including photographs, negatives, and other materials preserving UNK athletics and activities from 1960 to 1990. In 1977 Briggs served on the first selection committee of the UNK Athletic Hall of Fame and was himself inducted into the Athletic Hall of Fame in 1991. He received a Distinguished Alumni Service Award and a Distinguished Alumni Award in 1984 and 1993, respectively.

Joyce Iverson of Bridgeport

and held monthly meetings open to all members of the college academic community. In 1989 the Faculty Senate played an especially important role on behalf of the faculty when Senator Jerome Warner asked the members to vote on merging KSC into the university system.

When faculty compensation and benefits fell seriously behind comparable institutions, the need arose for a united faculty voice on issues concerning the work environment, economic security, and legal support. The Faculty Senate Welfare committee struggled with this issue for several years but was limited to making recommendations to the administration. The passage of the Taylor Law in 1967 had provided faculty the right to organize for collective bargaining and to exchange the right to strike with mandatory arbitration. In the early 1970s the faculty voted to join ranks with the National Education Association/Nebraska State Education Association. In 1972 with the NSEA's support, Larry Theye, speech professor, led the formation of the Kearney State College Education Association. Peru, Wayne, and Chadron State Colleges followed suit, and the four state colleges formed the Higher Education Association of Nebraska to bargain with the State College Board of Trustees. When Chadron chose to leave HEAN, the remaining three colleges reaffiliated as the State College Education Association.

In 1971 under pressure from the board of trustees and after 10 years as president of KSC, Hassel resigned and accepted a position in administration at the University of Nebraska. A nationwide search involving faculty, students, administration, and alumni chose Brendan McDonald to become the sixth president of KSC in 1972, and Dr. Marvin Knittel, who had served as acting president, assumed the new position of academic vice president.

Enrollments began to decline from 1973 to 1975 when students became discouraged by the limited facilities. McDonald and his administration faced a high vacancy rate in the residence halls as well as the need to cut faculty positions in order to stay within the allocated funding. However, this did not hamper KSC's growth, and by 1977 student numbers increased to a new high of 6,126, and residence halls exceeded capacity. Enrollments continued to grow into the 1980s. With a record enrollment of 8,000 in 1984, computer terminals replaced the old punch card system and speeded up the registration process.

President McDonald resigned in 1982 to return to Minnesota as president of St. Cloud State University. During his presidency at KSC, a bridge constructed across the 26th Street tailrace of the canal joined the two campuses and connected to Highway 30, allowing easier access to the campus from the west.

26th Street bridge joining the two campuses

Propelled by the opening of Interstate 80 between Grand Island and Kearney in 1963, the city, too, hurtled into a new era filled with ups and downs. The city's growth paralleled KSC's expansion; between 1960 and 1990, the population grew from 14,125 to 24,396, including a 35 percent increase in the 1960s alone. Many tourist-related businesses pulled Kearney south, including three motels, seven gas stations, and numerous restaurants, while a railroad overpass eased the entrance into the city. Kearney began stretching north in 1962 with the addition of Unimart, the town's first grocery discount store on 39th Street, and Richard Young Hospital and the Hilltop Mall in 1984. Then the city spread farther east with the opening of Baldwin and Rockwell Manufacturing. A new fire hall and a downtown renovation project reinvigorated Central Avenue. Unfortunately, with this new growth much of Kearney's historic past crumbled. The 1913 Christian Church building on 25th and Central made way for a service station; the 1893 Midway Hotel became the site for a grocery store; Chicago Lumber Company, Kearney's

❖ **KEARNEY**

Halvor Niels Christensen ◆

Halvor Niels Christensen graduated from KSTC in 1935 and received his master's and PhD from Purdue and Harvard. From 1956 to 1970 he chaired the Department of Biological Chemistry at the University of Michigan after serving as director of the Department of Research Chemistry at the Children's Medical Center in Boston and chair of the Department of Biochemistry and Nutrition at Tufts University. Internationally renowned for his work on amino acid transport in physiological and pathological conditions, Christensen was one of the first to be awarded a Distinguished Alumni Award in 1980. He also received a Distinguished Service Award from KSC in 1978 and an honorary Doctor of Science in 1990.

first brick building constructed about 1871, became a parking lot; the First National Bank razed Fort Kearney Hotel for their new facility; a new public library displaced the 1905 Carnegie building; and new county offices replaced the 1890 Buffalo County Courthouse, saving only the metal buffalo head above the entry. A progressive attitude prevailed as the 1980s closed, and the future looked bright for both the college and the community.

THE CAMPUS ❖ GROWS

Growth epitomized the KSC years, for not only did enrollments increase but major land acquisitions as well as building construction and remodeling accelerated to keep pace. In 1960 the college owned 108 acres with about 18 buildings, and when KSC joined the university system in 1991, the land base had grown to 246 acres with 37 buildings.

The first building completed during the KSC years was the $700,000 Calvin T. Ryan Library. The college had been considering an addition to the Administration building to expand the library as early as 1923 and had recommended a new building in the 1940s. Despite numerous discussions and studies, the governor did not grant

approval until 1961. Groundbreaking ceremonies for the new library—designed to house 200,000 volumes and seat 900 students—finally took place in July 1962, and in August 1963, the 70,000 books and bound magazines had been moved to their new shelves, a labor of eight days.

The remodeling of the Memorial Student Union in 1963 and the completion of the Nebraskan in 1965 further enhanced services to students. An 18-by-56-foot addition to the union enlarged the lobby and added a television lounge, offices, and restroom areas. When food service relocated to the Nebraskan, the cafeteria space was converted to a game room. The Nebraskan, with seating for more than 1,000 students and costing $910,000, housed the food service, the college bookstore, and offices for financial aid, the KSC Foundation, admissions, housing, and placement.

Another major project at this time, the William E. Bruner Hall of Science, faced problems throughout its construction. The legislature allotted only $500,000 of the $1.5 million requested for the combined math and science building. This money was to be used only for the first phase. After consulting various legislative

Calvin T. Ryan Library

Nebraskan Student Union

William E. Bruner Hall of Science

committees, the attorney general, and finally Govenor Frank B. Morrison, the college received approval to begin the construction of the four-floor shell in 1964, but no funds were available to finish or equip the building. However, matching funds could be obtained through the 1964 Higher Education Facilities Act, so President Hassel asked the Nebraska Legislature in 1965 to appropriate $1.25 million to be matched by $699,893 of federal funds to complete the shell already under construction. The bill passed the legislature on March 31, 1965, the day of the deadline. In August 1965 the federal government notified the college that the grant had been approved, and Bruner Hall opened for classes on September 1, 1966, at a cost of almost $2.5 million.

Mantor Hall under construction

Centennial Towers West and East

Student housing also became a priority during the 1960s. A four-story 400-bed facility, Mantor Hall, named for former history professor Lyle Mantor, opened for men in 1965 and served as a connecting link between Randall and Stout Halls. In 1966 and 1967 Centennial Towers West ($1.6 million) and East ($1.85 million) rose seven stories above the campus. Named for Nebraska's centennial celebration, these two residence halls for women, each with 398 beds, featured a new concept—suites of two bedrooms sharing a bathroom rather than the large, common restroom facilities of the other campus dormitories.

After the library moved to its new facility and the first floor had been remodeled, officials recognized that major construction would be necessary for the Administration building to serve its full purpose. Because of inadequate maintenance budgets, a lot of deterioration had occurred over the years. The state fire marshal condemned the auditorium in 1967. Broken and bent trusses caused large cracks to spread across the third floor ceiling and walls, where dated pencil marks proved that the walls were sliding, not just spreading apart. The college closed the auditorium and demolished it in 1968.

In 1969 when the legislature did not approve the $1.5 million needed to remodel the Administration building, which would have incorporated the north and south wings into a new central section, the college decided that a new building should be constructed. The Board of Trustees agreed in 1973. However, the state had closed the Nebraska State Hospital for the Tuberculous, now West Campus, and transferred 17 acres of land and 6 buildings to the State College Board of Trustees in July 1972 for use by KSC. Before any funding could be approved, the college had to assess how it would use the former hospital buildings. Meanwhile, the state fire marshal condemned and closed the second and third floors of the Administration building's north and south wings. By the time the legislature gave approval, construction costs had risen to over $1.8 million plus $220,000 for new equipment, an increase so high that only two of the three stories of the new administration building could be built.

When Founders Hall was ready for occupancy in January 1977, the art department moved into the first floor, and the economics, history, political science, psychology, and sociology departments as well as the School of Education occupied the second floor. Classes for these departments, however, were held throughout campus. The opening of Founders Hall made up for the closing of the second and third floors of the Administration Building, but the campus administrative offices remained on the first floor.

Ewald "Eph" Ehly

Ewald "Eph" Ehly was one of the most recognized choral clinicians and conductors in America when he received a Distinguished Alumni Award in 1980. A 1958 graduate of KSTC, Ehly earned a Master of Music degree from George Peabody College in Nashville, Tennessee, and a Doctor of Musical Arts degree from the University of Colorado at Boulder. He taught at the Conservatory of Music at the University of Missouri-Kansas City for 27 years beginning in 1972 and studied or conducted in the Soviet Union, Poland, Germany, England, Sweden, Denmark, France, Italy, Austria, Switzerland, and Brazil.

Founders Hall

Charlie H. Foster

Charlie H. Foster came to KSTC in 1945 as the only male in the Physical Education Department and the sole member of the coaching staff. As a leader in the area of women's athletics, he introduced women's track and cross country to KSC after his retirement in 1971. He served as a head coach in football (1945-1953), basketball (1946-1949), track (1946-1971), and cross country (1956-1970). His men's track and cross country teams entered the NAIA national championship every year he coached. In 1960 KSC named its new athletic field and stadium Foster Field in his honor. In 1968 Foster received the NAIA Track Coach of the Year award, and in 1977 he was inducted into the KSC Athletic Hall of Fame.

Fine Arts Center

With the demolition of the fine arts wing of the old Administration building, music and theater classes had been without classrooms for 18 months. When the Fine Arts Center opened in 1970, after 18 months of construction, it provided, in addition to classrooms, accommodations for convocations, theater and music productions, a scene shop, a costume room, a band room, a choral room, offices, and music practice rooms. Unfortunately, the art department could not be integrated into the structure until a wing was completed in 1980. When the departments moved out of Founders Hall, the administration offices filled their vacancy, and wrecking crews razed the historic Administration building in 1984.

Although the original Administration building could not be saved, nor could 28 large trees planted by students during early Arbor Day ceremonies, a large, anonymous donation allowed the college to preserve the columns and arches from the second floor on the east side of the historic building. In 1986 Jane and Dr. Lee R. Smith, who served as the college doctor for more than 30 years, funded an entrance way east of Founders Hall that used the columns. The light posts in front of the old Administration building, a gift from the Class of 1916, were moved to the southeast corner of Founders Hall and remained to stand watch over the progress of the college.

The legislature's transfer of the land and buildings of the State Hospital helped to pave the way for more growth. The hospital, provided for by an act of the legislature in 1911, had opened on a tract of land one mile west of the city in 1912. The first hospital, known as the Frame Pavilion, had a capacity of 32 patients. By 1921 the hospital and its 33 employees cared for 100 patients, and a long list awaited admission. A new building known as the East Sun was constructed in 1925 and increased the beds by 30, primarily for children. In 1940 the

Moving a column from the old Administration building

Column entranceway east of Founders Hall

Light posts at entranceway southeast of Founders Hall

◆ **Donald E. Fox**

When KSC reorganized from divisions into schools in the late 1960s, Donald E. Fox, chairman of the Division of Mathematics and Sciences and member of the KSC staff since 1935, became the first dean of the School of Natural Sciences (1968). A professor of chemistry, he received his BA, MA, and PhD from Iowa State University. He was awarded a Distinguished Service Award from KSC one year after he retired in 1973, and since 1981, the Department of Chemistry has invited a distinguished alumni to present a Don Fox Memorial Lecture.

hospital added a center and west wing under the Works Progress Administration (WPA). Records show that 61,369 patients received care at the state hospital through 1958. In 1959 the hospital admitted 172 patients, and the 67-person staff included 4 physicians and 18 nurses. In 1971 when the number of patients dropped to 32, plus 42 mentally handicapped children, the state ordered it closed, and the phaseout began.

One of the State Hospital buildings acquired by the college, the Frank House, a three-story, red Colorado-sandstone mansion, enhanced the campus when it was placed on the National Register of Historic Sites in 1973. The 42-room (including closets, for that was how houses were assessed), Romanesque-style Victorian home on the west edge of the grounds, constructed by George Washington Frank in 1889, featured a 5-by-10-foot Tiffany stained glass window as well as hand-carved oak woodwork, two bathrooms, ten tiled fireplaces, and a third-floor ballroom. The original cost of the house, between $35,000 and $40,000, included steam heat and electricity, unique features for its time, tiles imported from Holland for the roof, and copper rain pipes. Frank's projects included the Kearney Canal, the electric power plant, and the electric street railway system. After Frank filed for bankruptcy, Dr. O. Grothan used the mansion as a clinic until he sold it to the state in 1907 to serve as a residence for hospital staff. Renovation began in 1974 with the restoration of the Tiffany window.

Since the hospital facilities were not designed for classroom use, an assortment of agencies first used the buildings. The nurses' dormitory—now Welch Hall, named after business professor Roland "Stretch" Welch—became a home for delinquent teenage girls and then housed the business department offices. The main hospital building, now West Center, accommodated Head Start and the Nebraska Humanities Council, and the college bookstore stockpiled unused and

Frank House

Main State Hospital building, now West Center

Milton J. Hassel

Milton J. Hassel, a 1941 graduate of KSTC who completed his degree while also working as the principal of an elementary school, returned to his alma mater in 1961 to assume the office of president. During his administration, the college achieved record enrollments every fall until his final year in 1972. Enrollments grew from 2,021 to 5,783, and the faculty increased from 93 to nearly 300. The campus constructed nine new buildings, saw the demolition of the Administration Auditorium, reorganized from divisions into schools, expanded and upgraded the facilities, and grew from a teachers college into a state college. The school awarded Hassel a Distinguished Alumni Award in 1980, a Distinguished Service Award in 1984, and an Honorary Doctor of Humane Letters in 1991.

outdated books on the third floor. The Kearney Day Care Center, a program of the Buffalo County Department of Social Services, opened in 1975 to accommodate parents pursuing educational opportunities or seeking employment. The day care center also provided firsthand experience for students majoring in early childhood development by allowing them to observe and work with these children. The nursing, speech and hearing, vocational and technical education, art, social work, and travel and tourism departments and the Nebraska Safety Center and Elderhostel programs were also housed here.

The Department of Nursing moved into the second floor of the West Center in 1977, and after a modernization of the first floor of the west wing in 1978, the two-story facility provided 12 classrooms, 72 offices, 10 laboratories, 4 conference rooms, 2 seminar rooms, 8 clinical rooms, 6 project carrels, and an art gallery. When the college renovated 19,800 square feet of the east wing in 1984 at a cost of $1.1 million, the School of Business relocated from the Otto C. Olsen building, and it became known as West Center. Eleven new classrooms, new computers, central heating and air conditioning, an elevator, carpeting, three entryways, and an archway revitalized the interior of the building while an atrium and a stair tower featuring an outdoor clock refreshed the exterior. Centralizing the business programs facilitated better coordination between faculty and students and allowed growth potential for the department.

The completion of Founders Hall, named in honor of the original faculty of Kearney Normal School, and the addition of open space after the demolition of the Administration building encouraged the college to close the street

Memorial Carillon Bell Tower under construction

running through the campus and unite the central buildings with a mall. Its centerpiece, the 74-foot-tall Memorial Carillon Bell Tower, a gift in memory of the George and Venetia Peterson and Elias and Mary Yanney families, was erected in 1986. The tower linked the past to the present by using replicas of the original friezes and columns from the old auditorium in the design. The art department restored the original friezes, which were then relocated throughout campus. The Memorial Carillon Bell Tower, whose melodic chimes electronically tolled the hour, featured 24 bronze bells cast in France that ranged in weight from 48 to 1,477 pounds. In addition, an automatic electronic keyboard, which could also be played manually, allowed a range of songs to chime from the tower. This began a campus beautification effort that would continue into the university era.

Another building of historic importance, the U.S. Post Office, built in downtown Kearney in 1911, complemented the campus when it became the Museum of Nebraska Art in 1986. The museum began as a dream of vice president Harry Hoffman and the art department faculty, who organized as the Nebraska Art Collection Board of Directors. The collection, designated to celebrate Nebraska's artistic heritage, started with three paintings by Clarence Ellsworth of Holdrege, who specialized in western art. Other early purchases included a George Catlin portfolio of 33 pieces and several paintings by Marion Smith, the school's first art instructor. The opening exhibition of the fledgling collection premiered at the KSC Art Gallery in October 1977 and showcased fewer than 30 originals.

The project soared in 1979 when the Nebraska Legislature recognized the works as the official collection of the state. Later that year, the National Endowment for the Arts provided funds to add works by contemporary artists, and by 1980 the collection included more than 150 pieces and was worth $350,000. The largest purchase was *The Woman in the White Wedding Gown* painted by Robert Henri

U.S. Post Office before conversion into the Museum of Nebraska Art

Leland L.S. Holdt

Leland L. S. Holdt attended KSTC for three years before entering the military in 1951. Following his discharge from the Air Force in 1953, he accepted a part-time job at Security Mutual Life Insurance in Lincoln and in 1971 had earned enough credits to finish his degree from KSC. That same year, he was elected to Security Mutual Life's Board of Directors and named executive vice president. He was appointed company president a year later. Holdt, also active in community service, received a Distinguished Alumni Award from KSC in 1986, a Distinguished Service Award in 1987, and an honorary Doctor of Humane Letters degree in 1993. Each year since 1998, the Leland Holdt/Security Mutual Life Distinguished Faculty Award is presented to one of UNK's finest teacher/scholars.

in 1910 and worth $22,500. Meanwhile, the board launched a statewide campaign to raise $2.45 million to renovate and expand the building and to earn a $1 million Peter Kiewit challenge grant. The campaign succeeded, and the Museum of Nebraska Art (MONA) opened to the public in October 1986. Receiving no state funding, a third of the art in the museum was gifted and two-thirds purchased through donations.

Remodeling continued to dominate the campus in 1983. A seminar center was added to Welch Hall as a gift from the estate of Clara Ockinga, a business faculty member from 1937 to 1973. The building offered a modular conference room and auditorium with electronic multimedia capabilities for university and business meetings. The offices of the dean of the School of Business and Technology occupied Welch Hall until the completion of West Center; the International Education offices succeeded them. Also that year the Student Union became part of the Nebraskan and was enlarged to include meeting and banquet rooms, an art gallery, a snack bar, private lounge areas, a television pit lounge, an atrium with video games, and an outdoor patio.

The designation of the library as a depository for documents issued by the Government Printing Office in 1976 and the steadily growing book and periodical collections required an addition that nearly doubled the size of the library in the early 1980s. The $4 million renovation and expansion accommodated 25,000 new books, journals, and resources and 1,250 students, with additional study areas and seminar rooms and comfortable new furniture. Cable television was installed, and the library was wired for computers.

Philip S. Holmgren

Philip S. Holmgren joined the KSTC faculty in 1950, and in 1982 he stepped down as chair of the history department, a position he had held since 1961, to accept the role of college historian. Holmgren's duties as college historian included periodically publishing a paper about the school and serving as a resource for people seeking information about KSC history. He had already published a history, *Kearney State College 1905-1980: A History of the First Seventy-Five Years,* in 1980. When Holmgren retired in 1992, he set a record for service by a full-time faculty member. He received a Distinguished Service Award four years later.

The greatest improvement was the Athena and Charles Mitchell Telecommunications Center addition to the library, which housed the new radio and television studios as well as new offices, classrooms, and a Learning Materials Center. Thomas Hall also received a $902,000 expansion and renovation in 1984. Containing the English, modern languages, and journalism departments, the building gained new windows, carpeting, air conditioning, and a third more space.

Computer technology arrived quietly at KSC in the mid-1960s. The first mainframe computer, an IBM 1130, a single-user, punch-card-based machine with disk storage, was housed in the basement of the Bruner Hall of Science and was used for student registration, record-keeping, and the first computer programming classes. The college slowly upgraded its computer capabilities, adding an IBM 360/30 in 1972 and in 1978 a Burroughs B1885, the first multiuser computer that could support 20 terminals and necessitated the first campus networking system. Continually upgrading and expanding resources, the computer center moved to the Otto C. Olsen Building, and by 1987 KSC boasted approximately one computer for every 32 students. The next year, administration deployed a new financial system, FRS, and in 1988 added a student information record system, SIS. An IBM 9370/60 upgraded academic computing in 1989.

KSC's development extended beyond physical improvements, reaching out to the community and to the world. The Midwest Conference on World Affairs began in 1964 when James E. Todd, the first director of the conference, aspired to bring to the college community a broader understanding of global affairs and a stronger commitment to responsible and informed citizenship. Speakers from other nations, often ambassadors as well as leaders from U.S. government, business, journalism, and education, spoke at general sessions and seminars. They also met informally with students, faculty, and

Students using early computers

Midwest Conference on World Affairs

Speaker at the Midwest Conference on World Affairs

Midwest Conference on World Affairs banquet

community members at coffees, dinners, and social gatherings. The two-day
conference attracted hundreds of KSC participants and students from area high
schools but ended in 1976 when funding could not be found to finance the
program. KSC reinstated the forum in 1988 and renamed it the James E. Smith
Midwest Conference on World Affairs after the KSC history professor who
revived the tradition.

The Alumni Association also worked to promote a sense of community
among alumni, students, faculty, administration, and the community. In 1961
President Cushing asked Don Briggs, the campus publicity director, to add

◆ Karen Kilgarin

In 1980, just one year after her graduation from KSC, Karen Kilgarin became the youngest woman ever elected to the Nebraska Unicameral. She resigned nearly four years later to become the Lincoln Bureau Chief of KETV-TV News in Omaha. Kilgarin returned to politics in 1992 to serve as deputy chief of staff and director of public affairs for Governor Ben Nelson. Recently, she was named the director of communications and publications for the Nebraska State Education Association. She received a Distinguished Alumni Award from UNK in 1993.

Alumni House

alumni director to his duties. The position was combined with that of the foundation in 1975. Jim Rundstrom, director of publications and journalism, took over the position on a part-time basis in 1978 and became the first full-time director in 1989, a position he still holds.

As it had in the past celebrations, the Alumni Association played a major role in the college's 75th Diamond Jubilee in 1980. They purchased the H. W. Swan home, former residence of A. O. Thomas, for the Alumni House, and listed it on the National Register of Historic Sites that same year. The association also began presenting Outstanding Alumni awards. The first recipients included Rae Weimer (journalist), Richard Mengler (judge), Mary Elaine Wallace (opera singer/teacher), Dr. Milton Hassel (KSC president), and Dr. "Eph" Ehly (choral director). Another major project involved raising funds for the electronic message board near the Health and Sports Center.

KSC celebrated its Diamond Jubilee with a myriad of activities. Larry Sawyer of the Learning Materials Center presented a 14-minute program featuring 650 slides that required 12 projectors; Philip Holmgren compiled a campus history, *Kearney State College 1905–1980: A History of the First Seventy-Five Years*; and the college planted 75 trees. Numerous campus sites were renamed or dedicated: the Edith Smiley Registrar's Office; the Miriam Drake Theatre; Leland Copeland Hall; and the Bruno O. Hostetler Greek Amphitheater. The Jubilee, which commemorated "A Past of Distinction, A Future of Promise," recognized the significant accomplishments of the college and looked forward to new opportunities.

❖ **PROMOTING KSC**

Due to the increase in enrollment in the 1960s, KSC reevaluated its marketing and promotion strategies. The Office of Admissions separated from the Registrar to provide information about the college to prospective students by sending admission packets to high schools, providing career programs, holding senior-day counselor conferences, conducting high school visitations, sponsoring information days in Nebraska towns, and directing summer orientation.

In an alluring 1965 pamphlet, KSC listed the highlights of the campus: 153 faculty members and 125 staff; 3,000 students each semester, 1,800 in the summer; eight dorms, six classroom buildings, and married student housing; a football stadium seating 5,500 and a basketball court accommodating 2,700; an indoor track and swimming pool; and a new science building under construction. Costs for a semester in 1965 totaled $445: $100 for tuition, $330 for room and board, a $10 union fee, and a $5 activity fee.

Not content to remain static, KSC continually sought to improve its programs. A final major restructuring occurred in 1969, which established four undergraduate schools: the School of Business and Technology (formerly Vocational Arts), the School of Education (now including physical education), the School of Fine Arts and Humanities (now including languages), and the School of Natural and Social Sciences (including science and mathematics) as well as the Graduate School. In addition, five new deans were appointed: dean of business and technology Floyd Krubeck, dean of education Leonard Skov, dean of fine arts and humanities Harry Hoffman, dean of natural and social sciences Donald Fox, and dean of the graduate school L. J. Bicak.

This reorganization, in turn, necessitated the creation of new departments and the need for new department heads. For the first time, terminal degrees were required of all department heads; those without such degrees were considered "acting head of department." As a result of this reorganization, the college could offer bachelor of science degrees in 1965. In 1973 the Board of Trustees approved the granting of the bachelor of fine arts degree, allowing students more choices than ever. To help students take advantage of these opportunities, the Kearney State Endowment Association, originally established in 1959 to handle endowments, hired an executive vice president in 1966 and added fund-raising to its agenda in order to continue providing matching funds for federal loan programs for students and for scholarships.

Academic growth at KSC paralleled its physical expansion. New programs joined the curriculum, and from 1975 to 1985, 14 new pre-professional programs, such a pre-meteorology, pre-oceanography, and pre-agriculture, added options for students. In addition, several of the larger existing departments separated according to specialization.

Pete Kotsiopulos

Former Kearney mayor Pete Kotsiopulos graduated from KSC in 1970. As a student and business administration major, Kotsiopulos served on the Student Senate and as president of Sigma Phi Epsilon fraternity and the Inter-Fraternity Council. He was also elected Outstanding Senior Man. In addition to his work in the community, Kotsiopulos has served on the Kearney State Foundation Board of Directors, the Alumni Association Board of Directors, and as chair for the Diamond Jubilee celebration. He was awarded a Distinguished Alumni Award from KSC in 1981 and a Distinguished Service Award in 1990. In 2005 Kotsiopulos was appointed University of Nebraska Vice President for University Affairs.

◆ **Mark Lundeen**

After graduating from KSC in 1981, Mark Lundeen traveled to Europe and the Mediterranean, where he was inspired to make sculpting his primary occupation. Now a professional sculptor, his monumental and life-size figures have been placed in more than a hundred cities and locations, including the Baseball Hall of Fame in Cooperstown, New York; Pebble Beach Golf Club in Carmel, California; the Capitol in Washington, D.C.; Pro Player Stadium in Florida; and the cities of Seoul, South Korea; St. Tropez, France; Rock Hill, South Carolina; and Kearney. The college presented him with a Distinguished Alumni Award in 1996.

SCHOOL OF ❖
BUSINESS AND
TECHNOLOGY

The School of Business and Technology, formerly the Division of Business and Vocational Arts, expanded in 1969 to include programs in management/marketing, accounting/finance, economics, and business administration/education.

After the restructuring the management and marketing department consisted of 21 faculty and offered degrees in aircraft systems management, business administration, human resource management, management information systems, and management and marketing. Most of the faculty for the programs and the department itself were housed in Welch Hall. The business education program, one of the oldest in the school, offered an office management emphasis, a two-year secretarial certificate, and three teaching endorsements: vocational business education, basic business, and marketing education. For many years, a fourth of all business teachers hired in Nebraska came from KSC.

In 1965 students could major in business administration in the Division of Vocational Arts with 32 credit hours or minor with 24 hours. The following year, students could work toward a Bachelor of Science in Business Administration, which required 53 credit hours, or a Comprehensive Business Administration degree, requiring 77 credit hours. It became part of the School of Business and Technology in the 1969 reorganization, and Roland Welch was appointed head of the department. Beginning in 1975, students working toward a Comprehensive Business Administration degree could select an emphasis: Accounting, Management, Marketing, or Personnel. The addition of these options sent enrollments soaring, but underfunding caused chronic teacher overloads, forcing faculty to teach 15-hour class loads with three preparations. To add to the problem, pressure to provide programs off-campus stretched the faculty even further, dispatching them to sites in Columbus, McCook, Broken Bow, Lexington, North Platte, and Grand Island. Through the years, the school began offering additional options, such

Business professor and a student

as agri-business, real estate, and finance, and added an office administration comprehensive major in 1981. The personnel option became human resource management, and the management technology program introduced the aviation management program.

As KSC expanded its programs beyond the teachers college curriculum, general business professors in the Department of Business Administration in the Division of Vocational Arts taught a limited number of economics courses. During the 1963–64 academic year these courses transferred to the Division of Social Science, and Gordon Blake was hired as the first economics professor. Growing interest in economics brought additional faculty, leading to the formation of the Department of Economics in 1969. Carl Lewis served as the first department chair, holding that position until 1990. The department added courses in agribusiness and created the Center for Economic Education. In the fall of 1980, the department transferred from the School of Natural and Social Sciences to Business and Technology and relocated to West Center.

Because of the growth of vocational/occupational education, KSC added a Bachelor of Science in Occupational Education in 1969 and created the Center for Vocational Technical Education in 1972. James Miller served as the first director, and the next year Lyle Colsden joined as the center program specialist. By 1973 the center expanded to include program specialists for research, special vocational needs, adult education, and GED testing as well as a Nebraska Curriculum Laboratory. Funded by a combination of state and federal monies, the center, the only one of its kind, served the entire state and was responsible for millions of dollars in grants to fund statewide equipment upgrades and curriculum and leadership development. Colsden served as director until 2002.

Also affiliated with the School of Business and Technology, the Nebraska Safety Center originated when Senator Ron Cope, Dean Floyd Krubeck, and Eugene Buck, KSC safety instructor, met in 1972 to create an organization that would address the high cost of accidents in Nebraska. The Nebraska Office of Highway Safety funded a grant in 1975 to do a feasibility study. As a result, Senator Cope introduced legislation to establish the Nebraska Safety Center, which passed despite the governor's veto in 1978. Originally identified

School of Business and Technology administrators

as the Safety Center in the industrial arts department in 1972, with the passage of the bill, it transitioned from a regional center limited to providing the driver education teacher endorsement and a safety minor to a statewide center with responsibilities for education and research.

In 1976 the State College Board of Trustees approved the master's in business administration program for KSC, and it became the first graduate program, other than teacher education, at the state college level in Nebraska. Although demand remained strong for the offering, it had to be phased out in 1980 because of legislation that prevented KSC from independently offering a MBA degree. A cooperative program between UNL and KSC instituted in 1979 replaced the original KSC program. However, since students had

◆ **Brendan J. McDonald**

Brendan J. McDonald, the sixth president, oversaw many of the changes that made the school's university status possible. Under his leadership, the school improved or expanded many of its facilities, including the Nebraskan Student Union, Calvin T. Ryan Library, and Thomas Hall. The construction of the Ockinga Center and Founders Hall as well as the acquisition of West Campus (now West Center) also occurred during his tenure. Although McDonald resigned in 1982 to accept a similar position at St. Cloud State University in Minnesota (where he attended as an undergraduate), he returned to KSC in 1986 to receive an honorary Doctor of Humane Letters.

to take primarily evening or weekend courses taught by UNL faculty, the program did not succeed. With 31 percent of KSC students majoring in business, KSC successfully lobbied for legislative authority to offer the degree independently beginning in 1985.

SCHOOL OF ❖ EDUCATION

Also in the restructuring process, the Divisions of Education and Psychology and that of Health, Physical Education, and Athletics combined into the School of Education. Paralleling this structural change, the School of Education assumed primary certification responsibility from the Nebraska Department of Education. The school continued to provide a quality program for aspiring teachers, but it enhanced continuing education and advanced degree programs for teachers, instructional technology specialists, reading specialists, counselors, administrators, special education specialists, speech-language pathologists, and school psychologists. The school also developed professional programs in recreation and sports administration and exercise science. In 1970 the elementary education department established a minor in early childhood education to prepare students for preschool programs such as day care centers and nursery schools. And in response to the needs of local schools, the college developed programs in educational administration, counseling, and school psychology. This triggered an expansion of partnerships with public schools, Educational Service Units, and community colleges for practicums and internships as well as direct support to programs in exercise science, recreation, and sports administration.

Speech correction classes began in the education department in the 1940s when John McGee established the program to provide speech therapy for elementary students who lisped. In 1950 Harold Ahrendts provided speech therapy through the Department of Speech in the Division of Fine Arts and Humanities, and by 1964 students could major in speech correction. The program moved to Thomas Hall, allowing additional space for offices and therapy cubicles for approximately 25 students in 1968, and Earl Schuman was appointed the first director of the speech and hearing program. The college purchased the former Lutheran Center near campus in 1970 and converted it to house the speech and hearing program. Three years later, through the efforts of Professor John Cochran, it received a grant for $500,000 to create a master of science program. The grant, divided over a seven-year period, provided funds for four additional faculty to comply with requirements for national certification and to enable the program to acquire therapy devices, testing materials, advanced equipment, and an audiometric suite for hearing evaluations. As more faculty joined the department and services expanded, the department moved to the West Center building in 1975.

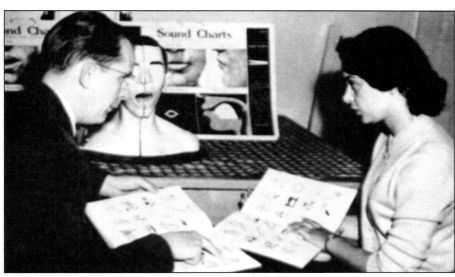

Department of Speech

Richard Mengler

Richard Mengler, one of the first people to receive a Distinguished Alumni Award from KSC in 1980, graduated from KSTC in 1933 and the University of Oregon in 1939. He served in the Army during World War II and worked in the Veterans Benefits Administration until 1949. He then returned to the University of Oregon and earned a degree in law in 1952. In 1955 Mengler was elected the first district judge of Benton County, Oregon, and from 1960 to 1964 he was also a professor in the School of Business at Oregon State College (now Oregon State University). He died in 2001 after serving as a circuit court judge in Oregon for 17 years from 1965 to 1982.

In 1978 the speech department began granting master's degrees. Since many speech therapy students worked full-time, the department offered graduate courses in the evenings and during the summer and increased their clinic activities to include the Veterans Hospital and Home in Grand Island, Bethphage Mission in Axtell, Good Samaritan Hospital in Kearney, public schools, nursing homes, Head Start preschools, and day care centers. In 1979 the program received national certification, and in 1986 speech therapy moved from the Department of Speech and Theater into the School of Education.

❖ **SCHOOL OF FINE ARTS AND HUMANITIES**

Throughout the KSC years, several programs shifted between departments. The School of Fine Arts and Humanities gained the Department of Foreign Languages in the 1969 restructuring. When it seperated from English, professor Betty Becker recognized the need for translators and interpreters in the United States and initiated the unique undergraduate translation-interpretation program in 1974. The department added two translation seminars to the foreign language curriculum, followed by a class in interpretation to form the basis for a certificate in translation-interpretation. Beginning in 1975, foreign language students could also major and minor in translation. By 1984 a course in English as a Second Language joined the offerings.

Over the years, the foreign languages department was involved in numerous activities outside the classroom. The Annual Foreign Language Day originated in 1974 as French Day for high school students but later expanded to include students of all languages. During the 1970s several study groups traveled to Europe and Mexico, but the most longstanding relationship began in 1979 with the *Centro de Estudios para Extranjeros* in

◆ **Jim Morey**

While attending KSC, Jim Morey found a career in entertainment. As the president of the Kearney State Student Council, Morey took the initiative to start a series of concerts that introduced big name stars to campus. After graduating in 1966, he took his talents to Southern California, where he and partner Sandy Gallin built the talent management firm of Gallin-Morey Associates. Over the years they have represented such stars as Michael Jackson, Dolly Parton, Neil Diamond, Patti LaBelle, and Mariah Carey.

School of Fine Arts and Humanities administrators

Guadalajara, Mexico. The international student exchange program began in 1982, and many Kearney students took advantage of the exchange by spending semesters abroad in Asia, Europe, and Latin America.

With an influx of new faculty members in the 1960s, the Department of English changed the curriculum dramatically. American literature, British literature, genre studies, and special topics supplemented the two general studies world literature surveys. Publications became a priority. Students revived the creative writing journal, the *Antler*, which had been published sporadically since the 1950s. Sponsored by Richard Cloyed in 1961 and supported by the English honorary society Sigma Tau Delta, students held writing competitions, offered prizes, and published the best submissions in the journal. The journal suspended publication for a few years but relaunched in 1986 as the *Carillon*. The *Platte Valley Review* was started in 1973 by English professor Ernest Grundy and history professor Gene Hamaker for the purpose of presenting a sampling of the research and creative activities of the faculty at Kearney State College. Vernon Plambeck became editor in 1976 and expanded the publication by adding special issues with guest editors and publishing articles written by scholars from across the United States, Canada, and Europe while continuing to offer a forum for KSC professors.

Throughout the KSC years, the Department of Music maintained high visibility. Both the Choraleers and the symphonic wind ensemble took three-day tours to cities and towns in Nebraska and surrounding states. Many student groups were chosen to perform at the Nebraska Music Educators Association Convention, including the concert band, the symphonic band, Choraleers, the Collegium, and the Nebraskats. The KSC Marching Bandtastics, created and led by Ron Crocker, performed during halftime at a nationally televised Minnesota Vikings football game before 60,000 fans.

The show, which featured the Nebraskats in one number and a special feature of the Wagoneers dance squad, was rated as one of the top five shows of the 1970 football season.

Theatre encountered a series of gains and losses during the sixties. A third faculty member in 1966 added a permanent technical position to the department. However, the demolition of the Administration auditorium in 1968 left the campus without a theatre building, so students staged productions in the basement of Martin Hall, in the facilities maintenance garage, and at Kearney High School. In 1969 students took three productions on tour to high schools across the state. By March 1970 the department was able to open *Oedipus Rex*, directed by Fred Koontz, in the new theatre in the Fine Arts building. Dance joined the department in 1978 with the hiring of Georgeann Spruce.

Theatre in the Fine Arts building

The speech program's annual weekend Institute on Leadership during the 1980s attracted leaders from across Nebraska. This gave impetus for the addition in 1982 of the organizational communications major, which focused on topics such as public speaking, small group communication, nonverbal communication, and rhetorical theory.

The broadcasting program continued its growth in 1968 when the student radio station KOVF received its FM license and became known as V-91. Featuring contemporary music and live broadcasts of men's and women's home basketball games, the students also broadcasted hourly the five-minute Action News, covering campus, state, and national news. The station introduced live bands from local bars, college talent, and special campus features. Four years later, after a fund-raising campaign on campus, the station added a $2,700 stereo transmitter, and V-91 broadcasted from 3:30 p.m. until midnight.

◆ Clara Ockinga

Clara Ockinga, the name-
sake of the Ockinga
Seminar Center, received a
BS from the University of
Nebraska-Lincoln and
an MS from Denver
University. She taught
at rural schools in Sterling,
Colorado, Bird City and
St. Francis, Kansas, and
Venango and Hemingford,
Nebraska, before joining
the KSTC business faculty
in 1937. She retired from
the college in 1973 after 30
years of teaching. Ten years
later, the Ockinga Seminar
Center—built on West
Campus with a $300,000
gift from her estate—was
dedicated in her honor.
The center was the first
building on a Nebraska
state college campus to
be constructed with
private funds.

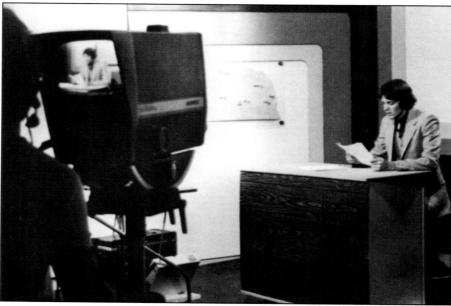

Student television broadcast

Television broadcasting premiered on campus in 1969 when a federal grant allowed the construction of a closed-circuit television station that provided educational and informative programs from Nebraska Educational Television, the commercial networks of ABC, CBS, and NBC, and from KSC's channel 6. Shared costs of program materials and preparations with the Nebraska Educational Television Council for Higher Education (NETCHE) enabled KSC to purchase new video equipment in 1975 and allowed the station to convert from black and white to color. The next year, KSC TV could be viewed on multiview cable television. And that same year, students could declare a major in broadcasting.

In 1984 the campus radio and television station facilities relocated to the Mitchell Telecommunications Center after the remodeling of the library, and the FM station boosted its power from 10 to 1,000 watts, changed its name from V-91 to KSCV-FM, and overhauled its image and programming. In 1989 broadcasting merged into the Department of Journalism, which became the Department of Journalism and Mass Communication.

SCHOOL OF ❖ NATURAL AND SOCIAL SCIENCES

Two major divisions from the KSTC years, the Division of Science and Mathematics and the Division of Social Sciences, combined to form the School of Natural and Social Sciences in 1969. Departments from other divisions also joined the school. The Division of Education and Psychology had formerly housed the Department of Psychology, and the program provided students with a fundamental understanding of general and applied psychology as well as the psychological principles underlying teaching and learning. In 1969 with Donald Stumpff serving as the first chair, the department instigated a major consisting of core courses in the history and systems of psychology, experimental psychology, physiological psychology, and applied statistics to create an identity distinct from education. Many of their electives, however, continued to be cross-listed in the Department of Counseling and Educational Psychology.

Upon the completion of Founders Hall in 1977, the psychology department moved from an off-campus house to the second floor, allowing them to consolidate the faculty offices, labs, animal colony, and classrooms. As the faculty and majors multiplied, the department increased the hours required for the major from 32 to 35 and introduced laboratory sessions to upper-level courses. The department revised its curriculum in 1980, emphasizing scientific methodology and adding interdisciplinary tracks, including comprehensive majors in human factors, psychobiology, and gerontology.

Social sciences classroom

The Department of History and Philosophy had become a part of the newly created social science division in 1939 and remained there when it reorganized as the School of Natural and Social Sciences in 1969. Philosophy was dropped from the department's name when the college hired Tom Martin to create a philosophy program in 1986. Political science became a separate department in 1970. History faculty numbers remained stable at 12 between 1969 and 1985, but deaths, retirements, and the authorization of new positions expanded areas of expertise, especially in non-U.S. history.

The Department of Sociology organized in 1971. Prior to this time, students could major or minor in sociology, but the high demand for graduates in social work and criminal justice caused an increased interest in the field

Kevin Rader

Six-time Emmy Award-winning reporter Kevin Rader received a BS in history with minors in social science and broadcasting from KSC in 1984. He worked his way through college calling KSC sports events as the sports director of KGFW-AM in Kearney and the sports anchor for KHGI-TV for three years. Now a political reporter in Indianapolis, Rader has covered such events as the September 11, 2001, terrorist attacks, the Oklahoma City bombing, and the Kosovo Refugee Camps in Macedonia. He won a National Edward R. Murrow Award, the nation's highest honor for broadcast writing, in 2003 for a composite of his work throughout 2002.

and the need for a specialized department. By 1975 five full-time and one part-time faculty taught courses that responded to the rapid growth in students' needs for research skills and abilities to enter graduate school. Social work and criminal justice eventually evolved into independent departments as well.

The origin of the Department of Criminal Justice dates back to 1973 when student interest and seed money from the U.S. Department of Justice prompted university administrators to create a minor in criminal justice. Housed within the Department of Sociology for two years, rapid enrollment increases expanded the minor into an academic major by 1975 when Robert Kaffer was appointed as the first director. In 1989 the criminal justice department formed and contained the largest number of majors of any single academic discipline in the School of Natural and Social Sciences. That same year it began hosting the Annual Criminal Justice Conference featuring prominent criminal justice authorities from across the nation. The department also launched its European Criminal Justice Study Tour in the summer of 1990.

Although the original 1905 faculty included mathematics instructors, the Department of Mathematics did not grow beyond two full-time professors until 1956. However, in the early 1960s and 1970s with the addition of statistics and computer science curricula, the department grew rapidly. In 1985 the seven full-time computer science faculty created their own program while the remaining seven formed the Department of Mathematics and Statistics. Two years later, mathematics had grown to 12 full-time positions with 2 teaching in the area of statistics. The department was one of the first to offer non-teaching degrees; the comprehensive major in mathematics was first offered in 1969, the computer science major in 1972, and the statistics major in 1975. It was also the first to offer a master of science in education.

With the reorganization of the schools and the influx of new faculty, new students, new departments, and new programs, KSC needed a method to analyze the progress and success of each department. Campuswide faculty evaluation by students of non-tenured and new teachers was implemented in 1980. By 1982 such appraisals, using a system developed at Kansas State University, became mandatory for all faculty; however, because of the expense of administering the assessments, instructors chose only one class for the evaluation. In addition, colleagues and administrators also evaluated faculty mem-

Science student working on an experiment

Lab in the School of Natural and Social Sciences

bers. By the end of the KSC era, the college had implemented a marketing strategy, a fund-raising program, a reorganized departmental infrastructure, and a tool to enhance teaching and improve student performance. Revitalized, the college geared up for the challenges ahead.

❖ **CULTURAL REVOLUTION**

College students in the sixties and seventies wanted change, especially from the conservative thinking of their fifties-generation parents. Political, educational, and cultural revolutions affected students across the United States, and although KSC did not witness the explosive events of larger campuses, the increased influence of the civil rights and women's movements and the Vietnam War protests prompted transformations in student values and lifestyles.

In reaction to the nationwide rallies, KSC students passed the Students' Bill of Rights during the 1970–71 academic year. First drafted by students Kathy Morrison, Lonnie Webb, and Pat Harrington, revised, and later accepted by the Faculty Senate, the administration, and 94 percent of the student body (by vote), the document mandated that student performance would be evaluated solely on an academic basis, not on opinions or conduct in matters unrelated to academic standards. In addition, students' personal or disciplinary information would be kept separate from transcripts of academic records, and students would be free to organize and join any associations to promote their common interests. Although they had to obey all college prohibitions of alcoholic beverages, drugs, firearms, fireworks, and explosives on campus while residing in college housing, students would enjoy security from search and seizure. According to an *Antelope* editorial, the bill of rights contained no radical statements because the KSC administration had been quite liberal and conscientious of student needs and requests and because the Student Senate had been careful about conflicting with institutional policies. At the same time, students also approved the Student Senate Constitution.

Other changes occurred when the Associated Women Students' organization replaced the rigid Women's League that organized in 1921. Although the group still established policies to "provide for the safety and welfare of all women students and encourage high standards of conduct," women from each dorm elected representatives to serve on the council and the AWS Court, where they could appeal their disciplinary demerits if they felt them unjust.

In 1969 AWS transformed the convocations and skits—formerly sponsored by the Women's League during the KSTC years to inform women of the rules and regulations of the college—into a three-day sex and morality symposium, SEXPO, whose purpose was "to afford students with the information

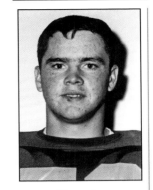

100 NOTABLE PEOPLE

Randy Rasmussen

Randy Rasmussen, a graduate of Elba High School, had never played in an 11-man football game when he came to Kearney in 1963 to play for the KSC team. Nonetheless, he quickly excelled, earning four letters in football, two letters in track, and All-NAIA national honorable mention honors for football his senior year. He was then selected by the New York Jets in the 12th round of the NFL draft and went on to start for the team as an offensive guard his rookie season. He stayed with the Jets for 15 years and played in the 1969 Super Bowl. He was inducted into the UNK Athletic Hall of Fame in 1980.

and thought provoking ideas that will help them better understand themselves and to assess their moral values as adults." AWS announced that it hoped to bring the questions of sex and morality from "behind closed doors into open discussion." Dr. Donald Cooper, director of Oklahoma State University's Health Center, presented the keynote address, "What's with Sex?" Other panels involving community leaders, health professionals, and clergymen discussed human sexuality, birth control, sex in marriage, venereal disease, choosing a mate, homosexuality, sex and the law (abortion and adoption), and the ethics of sex.

Student Health Services also responded to these changing lifestyles influenced by the drug culture and the availability of the birth control pill. However, injuries, burns, accidents, and upper respiratory problems remained the most common complaints. Health services moved to the Memorial Student Union in 1984, and local doctors from Kearney Clinic provided care on a rotating basis.

In addition, students, rather than the administration, began compiling the *Student Handbook*. In the 1960s the college had insisted that students dress traditionally in class and in the library, slacks for men and skirts or dresses for women, but after class and during labs students could wear casual clothes, slacks, and clean sweatshirts. "Dress up" attire was still expected in the dining hall on Sundays and Wednesdays. In 1965 the Student Council set new standards that allowed men to wear long jeans, if neatly pressed, but women still had to wear skirts or dresses. During late afternoons or on weekends, women could go out in "pedal pushers" or Bermuda shorts; however, cutoff jeans or short shorts were only acceptable in residence halls. By the 1970s both men and women students changed into bell-bottom jeans, fringed cutoffs, t-shirts with slogans, tank tops, and sandals or even went barefooted; men's hair grew long, and women's skirts became shorter. Information on pregnancy counseling, venereal disease clinics, and drug-abuse hotlines replaced the handbook's moral and dress codes.

Clothes shopping in 1972

Studying in the residence halls

◆ RESIDENCE LIFE

Phyllis Roberts

Phyllis Roberts, chair of the foreign languages department, taught English, French, and speech at KSC from 1947 to 1975. In 1984 she received a Distinguished Service Award and in May 2000 was honored with a life-size bronze sculpture placed in a newly built plaza area north of Thomas Hall. The sculpture, which was created by artist George Wallbye and depicts Roberts carrying an English grammar book, was a gift from one of her former students, 1958 graduate Paul Wagner. A plaque at the base of the statue embodies Wagner's esteem for his past mentor. It reads: "Never ending are the influences of a caring teacher."

The most drastic change, however, affected housing. Originally, housemothers, like Eva J. Case in Green Terrace, strictly enforced college regulations and were pillars of authority over students not only in the residence halls and fraternity houses but in the community. In 1965, for example, women still had to observe rigid schedules. Freshman women studied from 6:30–8:30 p.m. on Mondays, Tuesdays, and Thursdays, maintained quiet hours from 6:30 p.m.–11:00 a.m. and from 1:00–3:00 p.m., and signed out if leaving the dorm after 6:30 p.m. If the young women did not return by 11:00 p.m. on Sundays and Wednesdays, 1:00 a.m. on Fridays, or 12:30 a.m. on Saturdays, they received demerits. Written permission from parents was required to be allowed to spend weekends anywhere other than home or even to visit the homes of boyfriends, and then the visits could not exceed the limit of three per semester. Moreover, the college only permitted women in men's or men in women's off-campus residences if it was agreeable to the landlord, if previous arrangements had been made with landlord, if the landlord had notified the director of housing prior to the occasion, if the landlord was at home while the guests were being entertained, and if a minimum of three couples were in attendance.

About this same time, occupancy in the dorms began dropping drastically, from 100 percent occupancy in 1968 to 69 percent in 1975. Dissatisfaction with the strict regulation of hours and visitors as well as required meal plans and the lure of the freedom, convenience, and less expensive off-campus living caused the exodus. A new Key System established in 1969 allowed senior women who were 21 years of age and who maintained a C average to

Fran Scott

Fran Scott, RN, became the first director of student health in 1965, immediately after receiving a BA from KSC. For more than two decades, she oversaw a staff that included one full-time nurse, one part-time nurse, and one secretary. They administered to a student population that more than doubled during her tenure. She continued in her post for 21 years until her retirement in 1986.

Socializing in the residence halls

check out before 7 p.m. and check in the next morning by 9 a.m.—but even the extension of these privileges the next year to any 20-year-old woman who kept a C average—did not satisfy women students.

The college adjusted by making living on campus more attractive. In 1973 KSC initiated a six-step plan, using student suggestions as well as observations of other campuses to improve the quality of life in the residence halls, to allow students to express their individuality in their living quarters, and to make the program fiscally sound. Students could paint their rooms any color and arrange their furniture as they wished. Recreational and hobby equipment enlivened the lounges, new washers and dryers made doing laundry more convenient, and men and women could work as receptionists in each others' halls. The college also began optional housing programs by offering students choices in room and board contracts and relaxed the dormitory regulations. By 1974 married couples, usually graduate students, replaced most housemothers as residence hall supervisors. The dorms filled to capacity by 1980.

STUDENT ❖ ACTIVITIES

Educational, service, and social organizations also enticed students to KSC. The Home Economics Club, with over 100 members, became the largest organization on campus in the sixties. In 1966 students interested in aviation created the Flying Club, while more daring men and women formed the Sport Parachute Club. The Rifle and Pistol Club competed in 1971 in several matches with other schools, and the Rodeo Club hosted rodeos.

Between 1973 and 1985 the Student Activities Council sponsored many famous performers who entertained KSC students, including John Denver, Johnny Cash, Paul Harvey, *Star Wars*' Darth Vader, Cheap Trick, Barry Manilow, David Brenner, Waylon Jennings, M*A*S*H star Larry Linville, and Fritz Freleng, the creator of Bugs Bunny, Daffy Duck, and the Pink Panther.

Rodeo Club

John Denver

James E. Smith ◆

Flags flew at half-mast on campus and spectators stood for a moment of silence at a KSC basketball game in January 1987 to honor the passing of history professor and administrative assistant to the president James E. Smith. A graduate of West Point Military Academy and a member of the faculty for 20 years, Smith served as an unofficial liaison between the ROTC and the history department and took responsibility for teaching military history courses. He was instrumental in reviving the World Affairs Conference at KSC, which was canceled in 1976 due to a lack of funding but later reinstated and renamed the James E. Smith Midwest Conference on World Affairs in his honor.

During the early KSC years, women had the choice of pledging one of five nationally affiliated sororities: Alpha Phi, Alpha Xi Delta, Chi Omega, Delta Zeta, and Gamma Phi Beta. Although Delta Zeta disbanded in 1968 and Alpha Xi Delta in 1969, several new sororities originated on campus to take their place. In 1967 five women organized Phi Sigma Phi. After participating in formal and open rush in the fall of 1968, the membership

SPURS service organization members

Alpha Phi Omega service ftraternity

numbered 56, and the group was able to colonize in 1969 with the national sorority Alpha Omicron Pi. In 1977 Kappa Sigma organized because they felt that the existing sororities could not accommodate the large number of women interesting in pledging. They were the only local chapter on campus. Phi Beta Chi began in 1986.

Fraternities, too, flourished. A movement to affiliate with national organizations peaked in the 1960s. In 1965 the Caledonians, organized in 1916, went national with Sigma Phi Epsilon. Phi Tau Gamma, after 50 years of campus history, joined the national Alpha Tau Omega organization in 1966. That same year, Phi Phi Phi (Tri Phi) joined the national Phi Delta Theta organization.

More fraternities joined the campus in the early years of KSC. Phi Kappa Tau was established in 1965 and was nationally chartered in 1966; Beta Sigma Psi, a fraternity for Lutheran men, assembled from 1966 to 1987; and Tau Rho began in 1968, becoming Alpha Kappa Lambda from 1970 to 1973, when they disbanded. Omega Delta Pi organized in 1956 and became part of national Theta Chi in 1965. In 1966 Theta Chi introduced Big Bertha, a 27-millimeter anti-tank gun, at the Hastings football game. From then on, fans expected Big Bertha to fire in celebration of Loper touchdowns at all home football games. Theta Chi disbanded on campus in 1970. Acacia, composed of national DeMolay men, received its national charter in 1971 but disbanded in 1974, and Pi Kappa Alpha, President Nester's fraternity, chartered on campus in 1986.

A new national service fraternity, Alpha Phi Omega, following the principles of the Boy Scouts of America, originated a chapter and provided a large range of public service opportunities, including fund-raising work for the Muscular Dystrophy Association. The chapter raised so much money in the 1980s that for several years they personally handed Jerry Lewis a check on national television.

Throughout the turmoil of three decades, KSC adapted to student needs, relaxing regulations, and offering a rich and varied social life to complement a progressively diversified curriculum.

Charlie Foster coaching

Wayne Smithey ◆

Wayne Smithey, a 1944 graduate of KSTC, joined the staff of the Ford Motor Company in 1958 and was appointed the company's vice president of Washington Affairs in 1976. While a student at KSTC, he served as president of his sophomore and junior classes. After graduation he worked as a member of the professional staff of the U.S. Senate Judiciary Committee and earned a JD from Washington D.C. College of Law (American University). A former member of the Kearney State Alumni Association, he received a Distinguished Alumni Award from KSC in 1990.

With the completion of Cushing Coliseum in 1962, athletes finally had ample facilities in which to practice and compete, and the college now had an opportunity to expand its athletic program. Spectators were greeted for the first time in years with adequate seating when they attended KSC sporting events.

If the 1963 football season was any indication of how well the school would compete under its new name, then athletes and fans alike had reason to be optimistic. The football team completed that season with a 9–0 record, ranked third nationally in the National Athletic Intercollegiate Association (NAIA), and lost only to Prairie View A&M of Texas in its first national bowl bid.

In track and cross country, Coach Charlie Foster developed some of the winningest teams in the state. In the fall of 1963, his harriers won their seventh straight Nebraska College Conference (NCC) and NAIA District 11 championships and slipped to just sixth in the NAIA national meet. They had finished fourth the previous year. KSC runners would continue to appear in every national NAIA meet from 1956 through 1990, placing second in cross country in 1959.

The following spring, Foster's track team won its 11th consecutive NCC crown and its 14th conference championship overall. Although KSC failed to defend its NCC championships in golf and baseball during the 1963–64 season, the tennis team did manage to clinch its fourth straight conference title and its fifth NCC title in six years.

CHAMPIONSHIPS

1963: NCC Baseball (tie),
Men's Cross Country,
Football,
Men's Golf,
Men's Tennis,
Men's Track,
Wrestling

1964: NCC Men's Cross
Country,
Football,
Men's Tennis,
Men's Track

1965: NCC Baseball,
Men's Cross Country,
Football (tie),
Men's Track,
State Tournament
Softball

1966: NCC Baseball,
Men's Cross Country,
Men's Track,
State Tournament
Softball

1967: NCC Men's Cross
Country,
Football,
Men's Tennis,
Men's Track,
State Tournament
Softball

1968: NCC Football,
Men's Golf,
Men's Tennis,
Men's Track,
State Tournament
Softball

1969: NCC Football,
Men's Golf,
Men's Tennis,
Men's Track,
State Tournament
Softball,
AIAW Women's Swimming

1970: NCC Men's Golf,
Men's Tennis,
Men's Track,
AIAW Women's Swimming

1971: NCC Men's Tennis,
Men's Track,
AIAW Volleyball

1972: NCC Men's Basketball,
Men's Cross Country,
Football,
Men's Tennis,
Men's Track,
AIAW Women's Swimming

1973: NCC Men's Basketball (tie),
Men's Cross Country,
Football (tie),
Men's Golf,
Men's Tennis,
Men's Track,
State Tournament
Softball,
AIAW Women's Swimming,
Volleyball

1974: NCC Men's Basketball,
Football,
Men's Golf,
Men's Swimming,
Men's Track,
Dist. 11 NAIA Baseball,
AIAW Women's Track,
Volleyball

1985 Volleyball

1963 track

Women's basketball

1969 baseball

1963 football team (NCC Champions 3rd in the nation)

Men's basketball

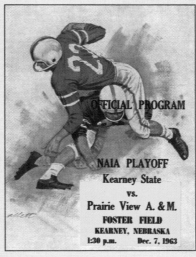
Program from bowl game

CHAMPIONSHIPS

1975: NCC Men's Basketball, (football), Men's Golf, AIAW Women's Track, Volleyball, Dist. 11 NAIA Baseball

1976: NCC Men's Basketball, CSIC Football (tie), Men's Tennis, Dist. 11 NAIA Baseball, AIAW Women's Track, CSIC Volleyball

1977: NCC Men's Basketball, Wrestling, CSIC Football, Dist. 11 NAIA Baseball, CSIC Women's Track

1978: NCC Men's Basketball, Wresting, CSIC Women's Track, Volleyball, CSIC Football (tie), Mens Golf, Men's Tennis, CSIC Softball, AIAW Women's Tennis

1979: NCC Men's Basketball, CSIC Football (tie), CSIC Softball, Women's Track, Volleyball

1980: NCC Men's Basketball, CSIC Football, Men's Tennis, CSIC Women's Track, Volleyball

1981: CSIC Women's Tennis, Women's Track, Volleyball

1982: CSIC Football (tie), CSIC Softball, Women's Track, Volleyball

1983, 1984: CSIC Women's Track, CSIC Football (tie), CSIC Women's Cross Country, Women's Track

1985: CSIC Women's Cross Country, Softball, Women's Track

1986: CSIC Women's Basketball, Women's Track, Volleyball

1987: CSIC Softball, Women's Track

1988: CSIC Baseball (tie), CSIC Softball, Volleyball

1989: CSIC Volleyball

Track

1990 softball

1981 women's tennis

1980 men's basketball

113 ■

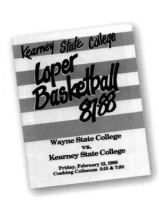

KSC won its first NAIA national championship during the 1963 season when the five-man bowling team, led by Jon Headrick, took the NAIA bowling championship in Overland Park, Kansas, by knocking down more than 11,000 pins in a two-day tournament. Headrick rolled a 621-point series. In 1963 wrestling become an intervarsity sport for the first time, enjoying a fair amount of success in its first season by finishing with a 9–5 record and an NCC team championship. Basketball was the only major varsity sport to struggle at the outset of the KSC years. When the NCC considered disbanding in 1969, basketball was the only KSC sport to have failed to clinch a title in the history of the conference. Throughout the 24 years of the conference's existence, KSC had so far accumulated 53 trophies, including 19 titles in track, 11 in cross-country, 10 in football, 4 in baseball (including 3 in a row beginning in 1966), 3 in golf, 5 in tennis, and 1 title each in swimming and wrestling. The NCC remained intact that year—it would not be officially disbanded until 1975—but basketball enthusiasts would have to wait almost a decade before KSC became dominant in that sport.

Cushing Coliseum also allowed for an expansion in the intramural program. Flag football was by far the most popular intramural sport even though male athletes had the option of signing up for basketball, bowling, cross-country, horseshoes, tennis, track, softball, wrestling, and swimming. Other intramurals, such as badminton, archery, wrist wrestling, mud volleyball, water polo, golf, rugby, and women's flag football, were either added or cut depending on need and interest. In 1969 soccer was introduced in an effort to replace flag football, which had been responsible for a number of injuries the previous season. Many students, however, would not be denied their favorite sport, and flag football was reinstated after just one year, with 21 teams fielding players.

Women's athletics, which featured prominently in the Normal School years, practically disappeared from the athletic program during the KSTC years. Except for the women's swim team, which began competing after the completion of Cushing Coliseum, and women's softball, which began playing a summer schedule in 1966, women's sports did not fully reemerge at KSC until the revival of basketball and volleyball in 1968, the inauguration of track and field in 1973, and cross country in 1976. Except for track and cross country, which were organized and coached by retired coach Charlie Foster, all of the first women's sports teams were coached by women: Rosella Meier, volleyball; Joan Bailey, swimming and softball; Connie Hansen, basketball; and later Mary Iten, track.

Many of the women's teams experienced difficulty scheduling games because of a lack of competition throughout the state. Female athletes also had to endure a number of prejudices regarding their ability to compete. Nonetheless, during the 1970–71 season, KSC was able to field all four of its women's teams in basketball, softball, swimming, and volleyball. In basketball, the rules were finally changed to allow players to move about on both sides of the court. Before the rule change, only two players were permitted to move about the entire area of play, although six players were allowed on the court. The volleyball team clung to a 16–2 regular season that year and finished second in the NAIA district championship. Although the men's swimming team won the NCC championship in its first season of competition in 1963, the women's team, as the only varsity sport available to women at the time, ultimately proved to be more successful. The men's team folded in 1976 after compiling a 1–2 season record, but the women's team continued to compete. In 1981 the women finished fourth at the first NAIA national swim meet for women. Two women were voted 1982 All-Americans: Marcia Konat, who finished fifth in the 100-meter backstroke, and Mona Lighthart, who placed sixth in the 50-meter-

1965 football

◆ **Jill Stenwall** ◆

Shot put and discus thrower Jill Stenwall participated and placed in four straight NAIA national track and field meets and won the shot put competition in 1980 with a throw of 51'1", making her the first female athlete at the school to win a national championship. Stenwall set new indoor and outdoor field event records in both shot put and discus during her career at KSC and was ranked sixth in the nation in 1980. She qualified for the Olympic trials that same year but was unable to compete because of an injury. She was inducted into the UNK Athletic Hall of Fame in 1996.

freestyle. Even though the team finished sixth in the meet, coach Joan Bailey was selected as NAIA Coach of the Year. The swimming team went undefeated, and six women qualified for national competition.

The men's basketball team finally rose to prominence during the mid-1970s and 1980s. Jerry Hueser took over the program as head coach in 1971 and quickly turned the team around, leading his players to 17 consecutive winning seasons. In 1972 the team earned its first berth in the annual NAIA tournament in Kansas City, and in 1978 more than 2,000 fans welcomed the team home from the same tournament as NAIA tournament runner-ups, having lost 79–75 in the championship game against Grand Canyon of Arizona. Hueser guided the team to the NAIA national tournament every year from 1977 to 1987. Their 11th consecutive appearance in 1988 set an NAIA record that has yet to be broken.

KSC won its second NAIA national championship and its first women's team national championship in 1987 when the Loper softball team defeated Francis Marion College of South Carolina 1–0 at Harvey Park in Kearney. Pitcher Phyllis DeBuhr won all five of the KSC games and did not allow a single earned run during the entire tournament. The win marked coach Brad Horky's 100th victory, and he was voted the NAIA Softball Coach of the Year.

In baseball, basketball, football, volleyball, track, cross-country, tennis, golf, and swimming, KSC continued to experience flashes of greatness and occasional moments of disappointment. The baseball team, which had showed so much promise in the 1960s, finishing with a 23–8 record in 1967 and earning a spot in the NAIA national tournament in St. Joseph, Missouri, had only three winning seasons in the 1970s and three winning seasons the following decade. Perhaps the biggest disappointment was the 1985 football team. The team won its final game of the season against Washburn University (Kansas) to end with a 3–5 record and its first losing season since 1960.

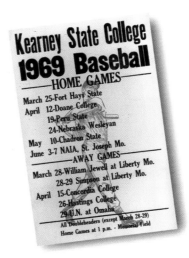

Roland B. Welch

Roland B. Welch joined the KSTC faculty in 1939 and served as chair of the business department from 1946 to 1973. For more than a decade, he served as a faculty advisor to the Student Council (Student Senate) and many other campus organizations. Better known as "Stretch," the 6'4" former college lineman retired in 1979 after 40 years of teaching and administration. In 1989 a building that had been part of the 1972 State Hospital complex acquisition was named the Roland B. Welch Hall.

TITLE IX ❖

A major change in the athletic program occurred in 1972 when Congress passed Title IX of the Federal Education Amendments. Title IX prohibited sexual discrimination in any educational program or activity receiving federal financial assistance, and in 1975 Congress specifically mandated the amendment apply to intercollegiate athletic programs. Although the KSC athletic program did not directly receive any federal funds (and could, therefore, argue that it was exempt from Title IX, at least for the present), it nonetheless recognized the unfairness in its current programs and committed to making its women's facilities comparable to the men's. In 1974 Jana Grundy played tennis and lettered on the men's team, but the college had no women's team on which she could compete. The new coliseum, less than 20 years old, was beginning to prove inadequate, for it had been built to accommodate a student population of 2,000 that had grown to more than 8,000, and an athletic program that had not included any women's sports but now comprised six.

The criteria by which sports received varsity status hinged on several factors: an expressed interest by students, the number of participants available to field a team, and the availability of competition within a reasonable travel distance. The sport also had to be recognized as a sport by some kind of conference and national standards. Because of these guidelines, only 7.18 percent of the female undergraduate population participated in varsity or junior varsity competition while the percentage of male participants was 17.34. In 1976 KSC conducted a self-study to look into possible Title IX violations. In the area of athletics, the school found itself to be reasonably fair. Only in the provision of locker rooms did the school find itself inadequate. At the time, Cushing coliseum contained two locker rooms for men, while female athletes had access to only one locker room that they had to share with physical education students.

HEALTH AND ❖
SPORTS CENTER

In 1981 the Department of Education's Office of Civil Rights appointed a four-member team to investigate alleged violations of discrimination in women's athletics, further prompting the school to update its facilities. Construction began in June 1988 on a $10.8 million renovation project to the coliseum. Two years later, KSC formally dedicated the new Health and Sports Center that included new athletic offices, four locker rooms, a wrestling practice area, racquetball courts, weight and training rooms, and a new arena capable of seating about 6,000 people.

Also unveiled in front of the Health and Sports Center was *Athleta*, a 20-foot-tall abstract bronze sculpture weighing 2,000 pounds and costing $90,000 from the 1% New Construction Art Fund. Built to emulate athletic

Athleta sculpture

motion as it swayed with the wind, John Raimondi designed it to resemble the forms of both male and female athletes in a variety of athletic poses as it greeted spectators to the building.

Despite setbacks, the athletic program ended the KSC years much the way it began, with drastically improved facilities and several programs on the rise. Having competed in two different conferences between 1963 and 1990– the NCC and the Central State Intercollegiate Conference (CSIC)–the school joined the NCAA Division II in 1989 and the following year began competition as an independent. Just as the 1963 football season must have seemed like a precursor to the success of the 1960s, 1970s, and 1980s, the softball team marked the new decade of the 1990s by finishing its last season in the NAIA with a second national championship in 1990. With 15 sports now in competition, including 9 sports for men and 6 for women, athletes had much to look forward to under the name of UNK.

❖ **CONCLUSION**

In his inaugural address on September 17, 1983, President Nester stated, "We may have been the best kept secret in Nebraska, but we will let it out in a continuing flow of communication, person-to-person, that does not reflect arrogance or competition, but the grace of knowing that individually and collectively we are a special college—one in which the citizens of this state are beckoning us to a broader and greater role in Nebraska higher education." He believed that through sound educational planning, quality programs, improved physical facilities, greater endowed support, and enhanced statewide recognition, "the institution's reputation for excellence in teaching would bring it to new levels of achievement in all academic and support areas." His words were prophetic, for 10 years later he would end his term as chancellor of the University of Nebraska at Kearney.

UNIVERSITY
NEBRASKA
KEARNEY

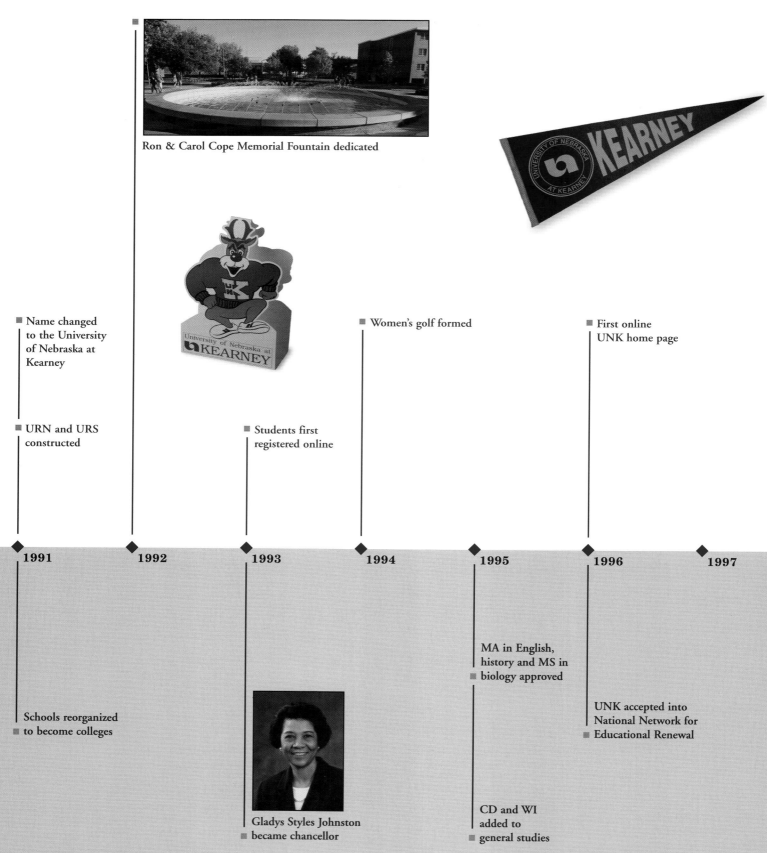

Ron & Carol Cope Memorial Fountain dedicated

■ Name changed
to the University
of Nebraska at
Kearney

■ URN and URS
constructed

■ Students first
registered online

■ Women's golf formed

■ First online
UNK home page

1991   **1992**   **1993**   **1994**   **1995**   **1996**   **1997**

MA in English,
history and MS in
■ biology approved

UNK accepted into
National Network for
■ Educational Renewal

Schools reorganized
■ to become colleges

Gladys Styles Johnston
■ became chancellor

CD and WI
added to
■ general studies

■ NCCA president
commended UNK
for its "success on the
field and success in
the classroom"

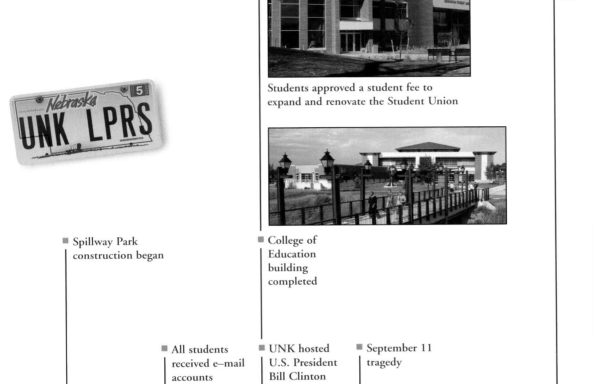

Students approved a student fee to
expand and renovate the Student Union

UNK Centennial ■
celebrated

■ Spillway Park
construction began

■ College of
Education
building
completed

■ All students
received e–mail
accounts

■ UNK hosted
U.S. President
Bill Clinton

■ September 11
tragedy

Foster Field ■
renovation began

1998   **1999**   **2000**   **2001**   **2002**   **2003**   **2004**   **2005**

UNK ranked
in tier 2 in
News and
■ *World Report*

NU began to
identify programs
■ of excellence

Clayton Thyne
became the first
■ UNK Truman Scholar

Philosophy major
■ approved

First UNK Student
■ Research Day

Douglas Kristensen
■ became chancellor

CHAPTER FOUR
1991-2005

❖ When KSC joined the University of Nebraska system, many transformations occurred. The president of KSC became the chancellor of UNK, the separate schools within the system reorganized to become colleges, and faculty had to reapply for graduate status. Admission standards increased, including the requirement of an ACT score of 20 or higher.

UNIVERSITY OF NEBRASKA
AT KEARNEY

T he idea of merging Kearney State College into the University of Nebraska system had hovered on the horizon for years. As enrollment steadily increased, Scottsbluff State Senator Terry Carpenter had suggested in 1974 that Kearney and Wayne State Colleges join the university system. Senator Gary Anderson of Axtell and Regent Robert Raun of Minden supported the union, but the state legislature did not grant approval. Another attempt to unite all four state colleges with the university, this time introduced by State Senator Peter Hoagland of Omaha, failed again in 1985.

Four years later State Senator Jerome Warner introduced LB247, co-sponsored by Senators Lorraine Langford and Douglas Kristensen, to make KSC a part of the University of Nebraska. Although the bill first required a study of Nebraska postsecondary education, it passed the legislature by a vote of 36–11. Deputy Attorney General Eugene Crump questioned its constitutionality since the Board of Trustees was charged to govern four, not three, state colleges, forcing the Nebraska Supreme Court to decide the issue. Although a majority of the Supreme Court ruled that the bill was unconstitutional, a super majority was required to declare an act of the legislature unconstitutional. However, with one vote short of overturning the act, the court declared the bill constitutional, and the name of the institution officially changed to the University of Nebraska at Kearney on July 1, 1991. Interestingly, Warner's father, C. J. Warner of Waverly, had introduced the 1903 legislation creating the original institution.

❖ **LEGISLATIVE BILL 247**

When KSC joined the University of Nebraska system, many transformations occurred. The president of KSC became the chancellor of UNK, the separate schools within the system reorganized to become colleges, and faculty had to reapply for graduate status. Admission standards increased, including the requirement of an ACT score of 20 or higher. The merger also presented the opportunity for the KSC Foundation to join the University of Nebraska Foundation. With the support of the larger NU Foundation, the UNK campus continues to see a dramatic increase in scholarship, faculty, and program support as well as assistance in larger capital projects, such as the renovation of Foster Field.

The Faculty Constitution and Bylaws underwent a complete renovation, adding a new executive committee and forming several standing committees. Since the Graduate School no longer remained campus-specific, graduate representation was dropped, and the formula for faculty representation changed.

❖ **TRANSFORMATIONS**

University status also affected the faculty collective bargaining association. The Kearney State College Education Association became the University of Nebraska at Kearney Education Association, allowing it to negotiate contracts with the University of Nebraska Board of Regents to ensure that faculty salaries, fringe benefits, and working conditions compared favorably with that of peer institutions. A new Special Master Provision in the bargaining law mandated that negotiations begin before the legislature set the budget, not after the lid had been decided and the session closed. Furthermore, offers on both sides would be comparable to those of peer institutions. As a result, UNKEA's first three contracts within the university system resulted in 9– to 13–percent salary increases. Through these negotiations, UNK rose from being one of the lowest-paying, four-year public institutions of higher education in the United States to one whose offers for new hires remain in the mainstream of the nation and whose professors rank now in the mid-range of faculty wages for its 10 peer institutions.

Even staff organizations changed. The original Office/Service Advisory Council—created in 1990 to serve as a communication link between the staff of UNK and the administration, faculty, and students and to promote a better working environment—evolved into a Staff Senate in 1995 to represent all staff employees: office/service, managerial/professional, and directors. In addition to recognizing employee of the month and department of the month, it started presenting the Staff Award for Excellence to individuals for outstanding service, established a mentoring program for new employees, and set up a scholarship fund for dependents of UNK office/service employees.

With the transition complete, William Nester retired as chancellor in 1993. From 1983 until 1993, he developed, improved, and beautified the campus. The closing of streets near Copeland and Men's Halls united the East and West campuses with the Cope Memorial Fountain as its centerpiece. His encouragement of faculty development initiatives and expanding the Pratt-Heins Foundation Awards for teaching, scholarship, and service encouraged members of the academic community to reach for higher levels of excellence. The number of graduate students increased by 25 percent, full-time faculty rose to 325, and enrollment had grown to a high of 10,114 students in 1990.

Gladys Styles Johnston became the eighth chancellor in 1993 and the first woman to head the institution. Although enrollments had dropped since 1991, classes taught by full-time faculty increased from 84 percent to 86 percent, the student/faculty ratio improved from 22:1 to 17:1, and the number of facul-

A young girl showing patriotism

President Clinton receiving an honorary degree

ty with terminal degrees, including instructors and lecturers, rose from 66 percent to 72 percent during her tenure. Teaching support strengthened with the addition of the Center for Teaching Excellence and the Office of Sponsored Programs, and grants for equipment-intensive disciplines tripled. Johnston also welcomed President Bill Clinton to campus in 2000.

Douglas Kristensen became the ninth chancellor on July 1, 2002. Even before his appointment, Kristensen impacted campus growth, joining with Jerome Warner in passing the bill moving KSC into the university system and playing a key role in the funding of the new Education building.

Douglas Kristensen speaking with students

Ali Amiri–Eliasi

Ali Amiri-Eliasi, a native Iranian, won two national championships for UNK as a wrestler, first at the NAIA national tournament in 1990 and again at the NCAA Division II Collegiate Championships in 1991. Eliasi also won 2nd and 3rd place at the NCAA national championships and was the first Loper wrestler to be named an All-American four times in his career. Eliasi won 121 matches at 150 pounds from 1989 to 1993. After graduation he earned an MEd at UNK while serving as an assistant wrestling coach. He was inducted into the UNK Athletic Hall of Fame in 2004. He now teaches in Florida.

❖ **KEARNEY**

University of Nebraska at Kearney

The 1990s propelled Kearney into a new millennium of leadership as well as regional and national recognition, and the city celebrated this growth in its 125th anniversary celebration in 1998. During the UNK years, the population of Kearney grew from 27,309 in 1995 to nearly 29,000 in 2005. Two decades of rapid building, from churches, hospitals, and schools to retail services, spurred Kearney's growth. An average of $57.9 million in building permits were issued yearly in Kearney between 1995 and 2004. At the same time, the city's leisure and recreational opportunities multiplied with the renovation to the Harmon Park rock and water gardens, the complete restoration of the 1888 Cottonmill Lake, and the addition of the hike and bike trail, Meadowlark Hills Golf Course, the 80-acre Yanney Heritage Park, and the new YMCA facility. Other attractions, such as the new Kearney Community Theater building, the Museum of Nebraska Art, and the Great Platte River

◆ Nick Branting

As a senior, basketball player Nick Branting earned three player of the year awards, including 2003–4 RMAC Player of the Year, Daktronics NCAA Division II Men's Basketball Player of the Year, and 2004 Division II Bulletin Player of the Year. He was also named the College Sports Information Directors of America Academic All-American of the Year for the College Division with a 3.94 cumulative GPA as a biology major. In 2005 he became the first player to sign with the Nebraska Cranes, Kearney's U.S. Basketball League team, a springboard for many players hoping to enter the NBA. In fall 2005, Branting will study at the University of Nebraska Medical Center.

Great Platte River Road Archway Monument

Sandhill cranes

Road Archway Monument added cultural options for students, citizens, and visitors alike while the Kearney Events Center introduced USHL hockey, arena football, USBL basketball, and big-name entertainment to area residents. Meanwhile, the annual migration of 500,000 sandhill cranes continued to lure more and more nature enthusiasts from across the nation and around the world to the Platte River valley each spring.

EXPANSION ❖ OF FACILITIES

UNK progressed, both physically and in the services it offered to the academic community. Not only were buildings added or renovated and the campus beautified but new and expanded programs eased students' transitions into university life.

Additional on-campus housing became a priority in 1989 when enrollment broke the 10,000 mark. The last residence halls to be built were

Dorm life

University Residence Hall South

Centennial Towers East and West in 1966-67 when student numbers first exceeded 5,000; now twice as many students needed housing. Eight 50-student residence halls, in the form of two four-plexes, were completed in 1991 west of the trail race canal to house the Greek organizations. Each cluster included an eating area with meals catered by the campus food service, a study area, laundry facilities, vending areas, and storage.

The Museum of Nebraska Art, located in the historic post office, was renovated in 1993, adding the Cliff Hillegass Sculpture Garden and an addition that almost doubled the museum's space. MONA grew into a cultural center that expanded on its mission of collecting and preserving art by providing scholarly, educational, and outreach programs. The permanent collection increased to over 5,000 pieces, and the new Skylight Gallery began to feature exhibitions by contemporary Nebraska artists.

Over the years, Copeland Hall, built in 1918 as the campus gymnasium, had gradually been converted to classroom use. A $4.2 million project renovated the existing space and added 25,000 square feet of new classrooms, lecture halls, and office and lab space. Dedicated in 1996, the

building houses the history, geography and earth science, sociology, and psychology departments.

In addition, the third phase of the West Center renovation, an $8.6 million project approved by the legislature in 1997, broke ground in 1999 and was completed in 2001. This modernized 91,000 square feet of the former hospital and increased its size to 120,000 square feet. Restructuring created 18 new classrooms, 15 of which are Smart Technology rooms, 7 conference/seminar rooms, 90 offices, 4 computer labs for student access as well as computer ports throughout the building, and a coffee and snack bar.

West Center

◆ Justin Coleman

In 2003 football player Justin Coleman became just the third UNK athlete to have his jersey (No. 5) retired. As a quarterback, Coleman set 15 UNK and 5 NCAA Division II records, including the season record for most touchdowns by a freshman (29) and most career yards passing (11,213). He threw a total of 99 touchdowns and in 2000 was the runner-up for the Harlon Hill Trophy, awarded annually to the best football player in Division II. The only other athletes to have their jerseys retired have been Randy Rasmussen (football, No. 76) and Tom Kropp (basketball, No. 50).

College of Education building and Payne Family Bridge

State-of-the-art technology also arrived at the College of Education in May 2000 when the university dedicated a new 50,000-square-foot, $9.5 million Education building. The faculty and Departments of Counseling and School Psychology, Communication Disorders, Educational Administration, and Teacher Education moved into the new facility. The office of the dean, 50 faculty offices, 3 conference rooms equipped with projection systems, and 8 large classrooms outfitted with electronic and computer-assisted teaching stations and wireless computer capabilities formed the core of the new building. Reflecting a new era in education, the building provided two distance-learning classrooms, equipped with fiber, satellite, and internet capabilities; two computer labs, each seating 30 students; 2 student/faculty work spaces for instructional and visual aids; 2 workrooms for student collaborations or meetings; and a 10,000-square-foot clinic with four practicum classrooms, 18 instructional spaces, 3 video supervision rooms, a technology demonstration room, a sound suite for hearing evaluations, and 2 seminar centers. A testing center for student assessment as well as national tests, such as the ACT, GRE, LSAT, and TOEFL, began to serve all citizens in outstate Nebraska.

That same year, the Nebraskan Student Union began its $6.3 million renovation that included a 25,000-square-foot addition. Completed in 2004, the new "living room" of the campus featured a 24-hour computer lab, stand-up e-mail stations, a coffee shop and expanded food court, additional office space for student organizations, and expanded meeting rooms for large conferences.

Complementing the new and renovated facilities, many groups and private donors added to the beauty of the campus. The Ron and Carol Cope Memorial Fountain, dedicated in 1992, combined with a new campus entrance and pedestrian mall to greet students and visitors. New works of art also enhanced the campus. A sculpture, the *Knowledge Tree*, was erected by the east entrance of the Education building. Its apple-shaped design profiles people who have influenced American education. In 2000 the university dedicated two life-size bronze statues that pay tribute to former faculty members Phyllis Roberts, French professor, and Don Welch, English professor and poet.

Student Union

Cope Memorial Fountain

Phyllis Roberts bronze statue

Don Welch bronze statue

James Cook

In 1997 James Cook, pro-
fessor of music, became the
first UNK faculty member
to receive an Outstanding
Research and Creativity
Award presented each year
to full-time faculty mem-
bers in the University of
Nebraska system who con-
duct research or perform a
creative activity of national
or international significance.
Cook, a pianist who
received his DMA from
the University of Texas, has
won several first prizes at
national competitions and
has performed in the
United States, Canada,
Spain, Austria, Germany,
Poland, Russia, Sweden,
and Switzerland.

Spillway Park with the Brad Follmer Memorial Gazebo

Construction and restoration of Spillway Park, begun in 1998, continued
to be a work in progress in 2005. The Nebraska Public Power District transferred the spillway property, a part of the 1882 Kearney Canal project for
electric power generation, to UNK in 1989. The first phase began with the
construction of the LeRoy Nyquist Family Bridge at the base of the falls and
the Brad Follmer Memorial Gazebo overlooking the falls. Next came the East
Plaza, featuring a 10-foot wall of engraved bricks commemorating Kearney's
125th anniversary, the Alvie and Ruth Payne Family Bridge between the
Health and Sports Center and the Education building, and the Earl
Rademacher Plaza. The next phase will include landscaping and the restoration of the old powerhouse into a history museum. Eventually, 15th Avenue
will be converted into a cul-de-sac that will feature a sculpture garden. The
2005 legislature also transferred to UNK land west of 30th Avenue on the
south side of Highway 30 that once had been intended for a prison.

Future building plans include the demolition and reconstruction of Case
and Ludden residence halls and the renovation of Men's Hall, which is being
saved because of its unique architecture. Case will be replaced first with a
projected completion date of 2007 and will provide 400 beds in suite-style
accommodations that will include a private bedroom, a kitchen area, a living
room area, and a bathroom.

NEW AND ❖
EXPANDED
PROGRAMS

In addition to new and improved facilities, support for special needs among
students became a priority of UNK, and programs were developed or
redesigned to meet their diversity. The honors program, which originated as

the horizons program in 1980, grew from 282 in 1991 to 461 in 2004, despite higher criteria for acceptance. In the early years, a minimum ACT score of 24 would admit students to the program; the average improved to nearly 28. Scores of the winners of the prestigious *Omaha World-Herald/Kearney Hub* Scholarship reflected a similar pattern, increasing from an average ACT score of 28 to 32 or better. The program also originated Campus Connection, a mentoring program pairing incoming freshmen with upper-class honors students, usually in the same major, as well as a student-generated newsletter.

To further aid freshmen in realizing a rewarding college career, the university initiated the first year program in 2002. Directed by English professor Kate Benzel, the program defined coordinated classes that work together to ensure academic success for new students. Student peer leaders (juniors and seniors) work with the first year faculty members in course instruction and serve as academic role models and liaisons between first-year students and campus resources.

Ethnic diversity also became an important focus. Since 1995 African American enrollment increased by 25 percent and Hispanic American enrollment by 10 percent. The Office of Multicultural Affairs was created in 2000 to meet the needs of UNK's increasingly diverse campus by offering a supportive environment for students. Curriculum changed to bring a more global perspective, most notably through the implementation of culturally diverse courses required for graduation.

For students struggling academically at UNK, the Learning Center was created–and originally directed by Kathy Carpenter–in 1975 to improve student study skills and provide peer tutoring. However, because more students with academic support needs enrolled at UNK and limited funding existed to expand services, the center joined with Student Affairs in 1993 to become the Learning Strategies Office and to take part in the federal TRIO program. The TRIO program targeted low-income and first-generation students as well as students with disabilities for intensive, individual services. By 2002 the changing needs and financial considerations of the student body required a cooperative effort of the Learning Strategies Office and Student Support Services, who joined forces to form the Center for Academic Success under one director.

The Counseling Center also continued to aid students experiencing stress, anxiety, relationship problems, academic pressures, homesickness, depression, eating disorders, drug and alcohol abuse, grief, and sexual issues. State-licensed and nationally certified therapists assisted students in making choices that promoted personal growth and academic success. The center also formed the student organization of Collegians for Integration and Accessibility to address the needs of individual students with disabilities.

Ron & Carol Cope

Ron and Carol Cope, both long–time supporters of UNK and active members in community service, have provided funding for a number of campus improvement projects. In 1995 the Cope Memorial Fountain, built through funds received from Carol Cope through the University of Nebraska Foundation, was dedicated in the middle of campus on 26th Street. Also named for the Copes is the admissions suite, the Nebraska Center for Safety Education and Research, Ron Cope, a state senator from 1975 to 1983, received a Distinguished Service Award from KSC in 1980 and a KSC Foundation Founders Award in 1987. Carol Cope received a Distinguished Service Award in 1988 and a Ron and Carol Cope Cornerstone of Excellence Award in 2003. The couple owned and operated shoe stores in Central Nebraska from 1939 to 1970.

In the summer of 2004 Student Health Services merged with the Counseling Center to form the Student Health and Counseling Center, directed by James Fleming and located in the Memorial Student Affairs building. Fully licensed and qualified nursing professionals in Student Health maintained their dedication to students' physical and health concerns. Kearney Clinic physicians continued to visit regularly on a rotating basis, and in 1995 Student Health contracted with Kearney Clinic for a nurse practitioner and added on-site lab testing and gynecological services. The beginning of Thursday evening appointments with a nurse practitioner from the University of Nebraska Medical Center in 2000, the hiring of a nurse practitioner in 2001 as clinic director, and the appointment of a health education coordinator in 2002 expanded the scope of the center. In 2003–4, students made nearly 11,000 visits, taking advantage of these services.

Also ensuring student well-being, the Department of Public Safety provided a full range of police, parking, and safety resources. Many changes have occurred since the 1960s when non-certified "campus police" carried weapons. Although officers have not been armed since the 1970s, all have been certified since the 1990s and commissioned as state deputy sheriffs with full police powers, including arrest authority. The 1990 Clery Act added new responsibilities to the department for handling victims and suspects, setting expectations on campus safety alerts, informing the sex offender registry, and enforcing drug and alcohol policies. The events of September 11, 2001, and the formation of the Department of Homeland Security further impacted the department. As a result, the campus formed an Emergency Operation Team, revised the outdated Emergency Operation Plan, and added a Safety Division responsible for the handling and disposal of chemical and hazardous materials.

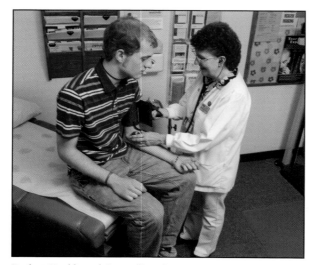

Student Health and Counseling Center

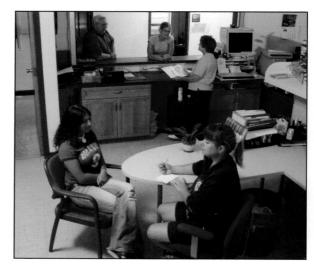

Public Safety

The Placement Office, now called Career Services, dates back to the tenure of Professor Del Danker in the 1950s when it simply served as a central location for student credential files, especially for teacher candidates. Today its services have expanded and the Career Fair, held for the first time in 1978, has grown into the largest in the state, bringing more than 100 engineering, scientific, and technical employers as well as over 100 business, government, and non-profit employers to the campus to meet with students. In 1977 the center began hosting the Educators Career Fair, linking potential teachers

Career Fair

Paul Fell

Artist Paul Fell, best known for his political cartoons, received an MAEd degree at KSC in 1973 after completing his BA and BFA at Peru State College. He joined the staff of the *Lincoln Journal* in 1984 where he worked for eight years. He now freelances his cartoons and has served as a visiting lecturer in UNK's Art and Art History Department. In 1989 he donated 60 of his cartoons for an auction benefiting the renovation and remodeling of the Museum of Nebraska Art. UNK awarded him a Distinguished Service Award in 1991.

with public schools across Nebraska as well as nearly a dozen other states. In addition, it initiated career assessments to help students decide upon a major and provides a database of 12 million companies with in-depth coverage of 30,000 of the world's top business enterprises.

Redesigned in 1992, the general studies program formed the basis for all undergraduate education and provided a broad educational experience. It emphasized a student-centered learning environment in the liberal arts, and it encouraged students to seek interdisciplinary connections and to apply their knowledge to personal development. In addition, it mandated that either within general studies or their major/minor coursework, students had to take 12 hours of classes designated as writing intensive to develop their writing skills and 6 hours of culturally diverse coursework to provide them with an understanding of the experiences and values of ethnic groups. Today students may choose from 170 undergraduate programs of study and 23 pre-professional programs.

The Alumni Association remains dedicated to UNK, working with programs, academic departments, and athletics in their relationships with alumni and in organizing alumni groups across the United States. In 2000 it created the Gold Torch Society, a mentoring and networking organization for alumni and undergraduate women. The association continues to carry on the traditions of coordinating Homecoming activities, awarding scholarships, sponsoring the Student Alumni Foundation, recognizing the 50-year class, and publishing a newsletter three times a year that reaches 32,000 graduates.

❖ **COLLEGE OF BUSINESS AND TECHNOLOGY**

The College of Business and Technology, presently composed of six departments and four centers, experienced a series of revisions and additions upon entering the university system. The Department of Accounting and Finance was created in 1991 with seven full-time faculty members and was responsible for accounting, finance, and real estate. In 1994 the department added

◆ **Dayle Fitzke**

Mathematics professor
Dayle Fitzke received
the first Pratt-Heins
Teaching Award for
faculty in 1981 and the
Pratt-Heins Service
Award in 1992. A 1951
graduate of KSTC, he
joined the staff in 1956
and retired after nearly
40 years of service—at
which time Fitzke was
presented with a Lifetime
Achievement Award from
the Nebraska Association
of Mathematics. Fitzke also
received a Distinguished
Service Award from KSC
in 1996, a Distinguished
Alumni Award in 1999, and
was voted into the UNK
Athletic Hall of Fame for
service in 1996.

business law and increased the faculty to ten. By 2001 required hours had increased in each of the emphasis areas, and the department discontinued the real estate option. The department expanded to 11 full-time faculty members teaching in the areas of accounting, finance, and business law with responsibility for two business administration emphasis areas: accounting and finance. It continued to provide business students with work experience for academic credits through internships with Kearney and area businesses.

The Department of Economics also continues to evolve, developing comprehensive degrees in business economics and agribusiness to prepare students for positions as business analysts, agricultural loan officers, crop consultants, or farm and ranch managers. The 2002 college reorganization moved the business administration/business education department to the economics department. From 1992 to 1996 the department had offered 7–12 teaching endorsements in vocational business education and basic business as well as the cooperative education/diversified occupations endorsement. In 1996 the department combined with the Center for Vocational Education, appointing Dale Zikmund chair. Currently, business administration/business education offers a BA in business education and in office management as well as an MS in Education in Business and Technology. The department also provides courses needed for vocational endorsement in basic business, diversified occupations/school-to-work, marketing education, occupational home economics, vocational consumer and homemaking, and vocational special needs. The business education program continues to be one of the top producers of business education teachers in Nebraska. The economics department serves the wider community through region–based research and

Student and faculty activities

active participation in the Nebraska Economics and Business Association.

In another reorganization of the College of Business, the management and marketing department separated into the management department with 10 faculty members and the marketing/management information systems department with 8 faculty members. Today management students develop skills to manage businesses, from small, local stores to world–wide organizations. The marketing program has undergone fewer changes than Management Information Services, but several new marketing courses have been created to provide more electives, such as advertising, retailing, sales, and research in both profit and nonprofit organizations.

The Department of Industrial Technology also changed with university status and no longer specialized in teacher education and industrial management. The construction management program administers the Housing Research Center, whose research applies contemporary building materials and techniques to practical applications for the home building industry. In 2001 students constructed the first steel-frame home in Kearney. Industrial distribution students prepare for careers in manufacturing sales or business operations while those opting for a degree in telecommunications management often seek employment as network, systems, and marketing managers, network supervisors and designers, or global data engineers. In 2003 aviation systems management joined the department. This 20-year-old program trains students to become commercial or private airline pilots or to manage aviation-related businesses.

Family studies and interior design grew to include two distinct areas. Family studies focuses on the interrelationship of families and society; human growth, development, and sexuality; money and time management; and professional

Department of Industrial Technology faculty and student

conduct. Students completing the program are eligible to become certified family life educators. The second area, interior design, enables students to understand the physiological, sociological, and economic aspects of housing as well as to specialize in kitchen and bathroom design. Students have consistently won top awards in national and international competitions, and the degree prepares them to qualify for state and national certification.

The college continues to grant an MBA, offering classes in Columbus, Grand Island, North Platte, McCook, and Kearney. Although Kearney is the primary location for the program, approximately half of the required courses are either available on the Internet or via video. When legislation became effective in Nebraska in 1998 requiring all CPA candidates to complete at least 150 hours of course work, students were required to complete a fifth year in order to sit for the CPA exam. The department collaborated with the MBA program to develop an MBA with a concentration in accounting that can be completed in one year. Several students in recent years have been awarded gold and silver medals for their high scores on the CPA exam in Nebraska.

❖ **Doyle Fyfe**

Doyle Fyfe played football, basketball, and ran track at KSTC from 1951 to 1955 and was the first athlete at the school to win 12 letters. Fyfe earned both a BA and MAEd at KSTC and went on to coach high school basketball in Nebraska and Colorado, where, in 1967, he was selected Colorado Coach of the Year. He returned to UNK as an assistant basketball coach and professor of physical education in 1970 after earning his EdD at the University of Utah. He remained at the school for 26 years and served as an assistant basketball coach for 13. He was among the first athletes elected to the UNK Athletic Hall of Fame in 1980 and was inducted into the Nebraska High School Sports Hall of Fame in 2001.

Specialized centers round out the current offerings in the College of Business and Technology. The Center for Economic Education provides K–12 educators with curriculum resources, offers economic literacy workshops, and funds economic education opportunities for teachers. The Nebraska Business Development Center, a cooperative program of the U.S. Small Business Administration, provides direct management and technical assistance free of charge to more than 2,000 businesses in Nebraska each year. Specializing in research surveying for communities, businesses, and agencies, the Center for Rural Research and Development assesses community needs for cities and towns across Nebraska. The Nebraska Safety Center continues to grow along with the university. From a one–person operation in 1972 to 8 full-time and more than 80 part-time employees in 2005, the center annually works with nearly 10,000 Nebraska citizens in safety training. The center continues to provide the driver education teacher endorsement program, and statewide services include driver education, driver improvement, evaluation of elderly and disabled drivers, emergency vehicle operator training, hearing conservation, and mine safety and health.

Enthusiastic business faculty

COLLEGE OF ❖
EDUCATION

With the advent of university status, the College of Education's focus on quality teaching expanded to include scholarship activities, external funding, and program enhancement to meet new standards. The college currently offers undergraduate programs for the preparation of elementary, secondary, and K–12 teachers as well as for careers in sports administration, recreation, exercise science, athletic training, and travel and tourism. Master's degree programs include elementary education, selected secondary education areas, special education, elementary administration, secondary administration,

College of Education classroom

speech-language pathology, counseling, reading, and community counseling. The college also offers specialist programs in school psychology and educational administration.

The undergraduate teacher education program, with input from a task force of 80 UNK faculty as well as K–12 educators in regional school districts, instituted significant revisions in 1999, and by spring 2005 the college had implemented new courses and hired seven new faculty members. The greatest changes occurred in the four-level professional education sequence. Future teachers now begin introductory courses as freshmen, participate in field-based experiences at every level, enroll in "blocked" cohort courses with English and American government, and study the role of diversity, technology, assessment, and democracy in public schools. Electronic portfolios facilitate student and faculty interaction with all records and assessments. Other key changes in the program included a total revision of the three undergraduate endorsement programs, a modification of secondary and K–12 programs, the merging of 11 graduate programs into 4, the development of the UNK and K–12 Partner School Network, and new assessment and site collaborations for student teaching.

The department initiated KASE (Knowledge and Assistance to Students in Education) to assist students in the advising and endorsement processes and the Alumni Ambassadors to involve graduates in advising faculty, setting goals, and recruiting students to the program. As a result, the college enjoys a 96 percent retention rate.

With the building of the new education facility, the Department of Communication Disorders, after being housed in five locations over the years, finally occupied the same building as the college to which it belonged. Its new home included a 10,000-square-foot clinic with clinical treatment rooms that could be monitored by faculty and staff from their offices, complete auditory testing facilities, speech and hearing science laboratories, an assistive technology center, seminar and study rooms, and offices for faculty, staff, and graduate students.

The health, physical education, recreation, and leisure studies department presently offers undergraduate degree programs in health education, athletic training, physical education, exercise science, travel and tourism, recreation and park management, and sports administration. Students can earn supplemental endorsements in strength training, adaptive physical education, and coach-

◆ Curtis Harry

Trinidad native Curtis Harry became the first athlete from UNK to participate in the Olympics when he and fellow teammate Gregory Sun competed in the 1994 Winter Olympics in Lillehammer, Norway. As the brakeman for Trinidad's first two-man bobsled team, Harry had made only six runs on a bobsled course before competing in Lillehammer, but he and Sun finished 37th out of the 43 teams competing. A former sprinter on the KSC track team, Harry graduated in 1988 and earned a master's degree in 1993. He again represented Trinidad and Tobago as a bobsledder in the Winter Olympics in Nagano, Japan, in 1998.

ing. MA degrees are available in adaptive physical education, master teacher of physical education, exercise science, and general physical education with specializations in sports administration and recreation. The department also hosts the National Youth Sports Program, a free five-week, federally funded summer camp that gives 10–16-year-old disadvantaged children the chance to participate in sports and educational activities that promote math and science skills, nutrition and healthy eating, drug- and alcohol-use prevention, and career and educational opportunities.

The Department of Counseling and School Psychology—with more than 200 students working to complete a master's or specialist degree—provides training in elementary and secondary schools, educational service units, college counseling and student life centers, private counseling agencies, drug and alcohol treatment facilities, vocational rehabilitation services, mental health centers, psychiatric centers, and hospitals.

The College of Education currently comprises 20 percent of the UNK student population, not including students pursuing degrees in secondary education in the arts, sciences, and business. Approximately 75 percent of all graduate students are pursuing master's or specialist degrees in education.

COLLEGE OF ❖ FINE ARTS AND HUMANITIES

The College of Fine Arts and Humanities continues to provide students with a strong liberal arts education. The Walker Art Gallery, named for Robert L. Walker, a Kearney banker who donated $50,000 for an exhibition hall in the fine arts wing, features student shows as well as regionally and nationally recognized guest artists.

The Department of Art and Art History has expanded to provide students with a variety of professional career options, including visual communication and design, art education, art history, and studio art. The newest program, visual communication and design, began in 1994 and provides one-third of the courses in the multimedia bachelor of arts or science degree. Students

Graphic design students in a computer lab

Drawing professor with a student

Students in the Walker Art Gallery

consistently win awards at American Institute of Graphic Arts competitions and work as interns throughout the state. The student-operated, nonprofit design studio, dpi graphics, originally known as IN2PRINT, creates logos for university and community organizations and helps companies with advertising designs, brochures, catalogues, and annual reports.

In 1998 speech joined the Department of Journalism and Mass Communication, which became the Department of Communication. Courses in desktop publishing, writing, basic speech, audio and video production, photojournalism, and electronic newsgathering teach students basic skills while upper-level classes focus on areas such as broadcast and newspaper management, organizational communication, media research, and public relations strategies. With the opening of the library's Mitchell Telecommunications Center in 2002, radio, video, and print media were housed together, and the department decided to coordinate all three to create an online, multimedia version of the school newspaper. Not only can today's students look at an online version of past or present editions of the *Antelope*, but they can also click on images that provide audio and video supplements to particular stories. Campus radio also advanced in technology, launching an automated computer system to provide 24-hour programming and web streaming of the station's programming.

The Department of English—in addition to serving students university-wide with composition and writing intensive coursework—has added a broad range of literature specializations. While the interdisciplinary language arts endorsement is the fastest growing area of the curriculum, students may also choose a writing emphasis major in addition to a new minor in popular culture. Graduate students can now earn an MA in English rather than in education, and in the fall of 2005 UNK is teaming up with UNO to offer the terminal MFA in creative writing. When Charles Fort was appointed to the Reynolds Chair in 1999 after Don Welch's retirement, he began the first Reynolds Writers and Readers Series, hosting poets and authors from across the United States, and he instigated the first poetry slam competitions.

The Department of Foreign Languages became known as the Department of Modern Languages in 1996 in order to recognize its more international focus, recruiting graduate assistants to teach beginning Japanese, Chinese, and Arabic along with Spanish, French, and German. The department's most notable shift occurred in the number of students studying Spanish, a national trend and directly linked to the growing Hispanic population in Nebraska. The return of Dr. Betty Becker-Theye from the dean's office

Marg Helgenberger

Actress Marg Helgenberger attended KSC from 1977 to 1979, after which she transferred to Northwestern University and received a BS from the School of Speech (now the School of Communications). She was discovered by a talent scout in 1981 while performing as Kate in a Northwestern University production of *Taming of the Shrew.* She went on to appear in several television shows, including *CSI: Crime Scene Investigation,* and has starred in several movies, including *China Beach* and *Erin Brockovich.* She won a People's Choice Award for Favorite Female Television Star in 2005.

Group discussion in an English class

to the department in 1994 reinvigorated the translation-interpretation program. When she retired, Dr. Eduardo González, who had been trained as translator and interpreter in Cuba and who is one of only two certified U.S. federal interpreters in Nebraska, joined the faculty in 2001. He created a second interpretation course and a four-semester program, raising the professional skill level and marketability of the graduates. The annual Language Fair continues to be popular, drawing more than 500 high school students to campus yearly for poster, poetry, and skit competitions, the College Bowl, and mini-lessons.

During the 1990s the Department of Music expanded to include the dance and theatre programs, and its name changed to the Department of Music and Performing Arts. Student performance highlights of the UNK years include Choraleers performances under the direction of David Bauer at Carnegie Hall and the Mormon Tabernacle and a senior showcase of musical theatre students directed by Anne Foradori in Chicago. Approximately 50 to 75 students audition each year for the 14 singer/dancer positions with the Nebraskats show choir, founded in 1967 by William Lynn. Each spring the Nebraskats, who celebrated their 35th anniversary in 2003 with a reunion, perform on a three-day circuit of Nebraska and surrounding states and have toured and performed in Chicago, Washington D.C., Japan, Germany, Austria, the Czech Republic, England, China, and Australia as well as for alumni groups in California and Arizona.

Annually, the department hosts numerous events, including guest artist performances, workshops, and master classes featuring national and world-class musicians as well as conferences, high school workshops, clinics, and festivals. To support musician-teachers, the department created a Music

UNK Symphony conductor

UNK Choir

Gladys Styles Johnston

In 1993 UNK appointed Gladys Styles Johnston, a former elementary school teacher and principal, the eighth president. Johnston, who received a doctorate in educational administration at Cornell University in 1974, had previously served as head of the educational administration department at Rutgers University and dean of the College of Education at Arizona State University. She came to UNK from Chicago, where she was serving as executive vice president of DePaul University. She retired from UNK in 2002 with a list of accomplishments that included a $6.3 million addition to the Nebraskan Student Union.

Pedagogy Resource Center and a music technology lab to enhance up-to-date learning opportunities for performers and future teachers. Concerts-on-the-Platte Guest Artist/Faculty Recital Series, featuring solo and chamber music concerts, and the annual New Music Festival, spotlighting the works of faculty, student, and professional composers, currently showcase the department's commitment to the cultural community.

Work in the classroom, on stage, and in professional settings prepares UNK theatre students for productive careers in the theatre arts. More than 200 different faculty-directed shows and twice as many student-directed performances have been staged at KSC/UNK since theatre was recognized as a program in 1966. Productions have ranged from Rodgers and Hammerstein's *The Sound of Music* and Sam Shepard's *True West* to Moliere's *The Imaginary Invalid* and Shakespeare's *Macbeth*. For 10 years, from 1989 to 1999, the theatre department sponsored the Great Platte River Playwrights Festival, the only original repertory competition in Nebraska. It premiered more than 30 original plays, bringing nationally known as well as beginning playwrights

from all over the nation to KSC. The department also reinstated the one-act play contest in 1997, bringing thousands of students and family members on campus as well as truck- and trailer-loads of costumes and stage props.

Theater performance

Rounding out the College of Fine Art and Humanities, the philosophy program, established in 1986, now offers both a major and a minor for students. Described as a "great books program," students study original sources of classic writers rather than textbooks and go on to careers in education, law, medicine, and government as well as graduate programs. In 2004 a $500,000 anonymous gift established the O. K. Bouwsma Chair in Philosophy.

❖ **COLLEGE OF NATURAL AND SOCIAL SCIENCES**

The renovation of Copeland Hall in 1996 allowed for the growth of many programs in the College of Natural and Social Sciences. Three departments—chemistry (1993), psychology (1998), and political science (2003)—have received the University Departmental Teaching Award which is given yearly to one department within the entire university system. In addition, three professors have earned the university-wide Teaching and Instructional Creativity Award: Don Kaufman

(1992) in chemistry and Richard Miller (1997) and Robert Rycek (2001) in psychology.

Grant-funded research generating nearly $500,000 and the addition of a new greenhouse, which offers space for both faculty and student research, has invigorated the Department of Biology. Another highly visible addition to the department in 1997 has been the Mobile Environmental Laboratory (MEL), funded by a $113,000 grant that allowed the department to purchase a 32-foot goose-necked trailer, a 4x4 pickup, and scientific equipment. MEL, with an eye-catching mural designed by Rick Simonson of the biology department, has covered the state, allowing undergraduates to conduct field research from the Sandhills to the Republican River valley. Faculty use it to assist communities in natural resource monitoring (especially water quality) and to present science demonstrations to public schools throughout the state. The department offers an MS in Biology in addition to an MA in Biology Education. New to the department is the innovative Distance Education Master in Biology, which offers coursework online and by videotape.

The Department of Chemistry offers an MS, certified by the American Chemical Society, to prepare students to become professional chemists. Chemistry students prepare for health profession schools and for careers in areas such as environmental analysis, hazardous waste remediation, herbicide/pesticide development, or in the chemistry business and sales management fields. The chemistry 7–12 teaching endorsement and the liberal arts chemistry degree are popular choices. During the summer, the department sponsors the weeklong Adventures in Chemistry camp that allows high school juniors and seniors to work one-on-one with chemistry faculty in labs and to participate in field trips to local chemical industries.

Mobile Enviromental Laboratory (MEL) in the field

Jack Karraker ◆

Professor Jack Karraker, currently the longest tenured professor at UNK, came to KSTC in 1961 and will retire in 2006. While chair of the Department of Art for 32 years, four new degrees were added to the department of Art: the BFA in Studio, the BFA in Visual Communication, the BA in Art History, and the MAEd in Art. When Karraker came to the institution, two full–time professors were on the faculty. When he retired as chair in 1992, there were 14 full–time and 8 part–time professors and 250 majors in the degree program. As head of the Acquisitions Committee, he was instrumental in the development of the Nebraska Art Collection and of MONA.

Because computer skills are being required for a wider range of occupations, the Department of Computer Science and Information Systems presently offers several options, training students for careers as software engineers, research scientists, applications and systems programmers, network administrators, and webmasters. They work with a broad range of hardware, including personal as well as mainframe computers, and have access to a CASE/UNIX lab and a special projects lab for teacher and student collaborative research.

Preparing students for employment in law enforcement, corrections, and the court as well as cultivating an understanding of past and present trends in crime and criminal methodology, the Department of Criminal Justice and Social Work continues to contribute the largest number of majors in the College of Natural and Social Sciences. The focus of the social work program prepares students for careers in child welfare and family services, youth residential treatment facilities, elder care programs, addiction and mental health services, domestic violence programs, corrections, and business and government leadership.

In 1998 the department instituted a cooperative agreement with the U.S. Department of Justice to use the Kearney campus for a number of important law enforcement programs. These include summer training seminars for local, county, state, and federal personnel from throughout the Midwest concerning gang resistance education for on-site high school police officers, community policing tactics, and the establishment of rural drug task forces.

The geography and earth science department caters to students planning international careers or considering environmental management and resource conservation careers. The department grants comprehensive majors in environmental studies, human/global studies, travel and tourism, and the new spatial analysis option. In addition to academic courses, geography students have con-

◆ **Don Kaufman**

Don Kaufman, professor of chemistry, received the Outstanding Teaching and Instructional Creativity Award from the University of Nebraska in 1992. He was the first UNK professor to win the award, two of which are presented each year to full-time University of Nebraska faculty members of at least five years for meritorious and sustained records of excellence in teaching and creativity. Kaufman received his BS from the University of Nebraska-Lincoln and earned his MS and PhD at Colorado State University in 1965 and 1969. His other teaching honors include a Pratt-Heins Award in 1986 and a Nebraska Board of Trustees Outstanding Teaching Award in 1988. He was also KSC's first student-selected Outstanding Professor.

ducted independent research projects with the National Conference on Undergraduate Research/Lancy Platte River Project while others have participated in internship programs with agencies such as the U.S. Army Corps of Engineers, Americorps, the Tri-Basin Natural Resources District, and the City of Kearney.

The Department of Health Science offers 19 health-related programs. Approximately 70 percent of UNK students in the department's various health programs have been accepted into professional schools and clinical programs.

After years of effort, the history department received approval from the regents and the Coordinating Commission to offer an MA beginning in 1992. New faculty have also broadened the areas of expertise in the department, offering specializations in American, European, Latin American, and Asian history. The department sponsors Nebraska History Day, a program that encourages high school juniors and seniors to research a topic of interest and develop an original paper, presentation, or exhibit. Graduate students, librarians, and UNK history faculty serve as judges, and winners in the regional contest advance to the state and, ultimately, national competition levels.

The Department of Mathematics and Statistics has faced dramatic changes. Due to budget constraints, the department had to discontinue the statistics major and the master's degree program. However, the department continues to offer five majors, two minors, supporting courses for a wide variety of other majors, and eight general studies courses.

The political science department offers a major and minor as well as political science and social science teaching endorsements, a major in public administration, and a pre-law program. Semester or summer internships also connect students to career opportunities in the Washington, D.C. offices of Nebraska senators and representatives, with international organiza-

Students working on a chemistry experiment

tions, in Nebraska state and local government, community and public organizations, and law and judicial offices.

The Department of Psychology began a curriculum revision in 1990 to add lab components to core courses in statistics, experimental psychology, and several advanced courses. The move from Founders Hall to the newly remodeled Copeland Hall provided the department with student and faculty laboratories and specialized lab facilities in child development, physiological psychology, and human experimental psychology.

Faculty and students in the Department of Sociology started applied research in several rural areas in 1998 because of the rising concern for the changes taking place in rural and small town America, especially in Nebraska. The department will soon be offering another emphasis focusing on global and international trends in society.

José Mena-Werth of the physics and physical science department continues to direct the UNK Planetarium. He conducts a variety of monthly showings, such as "The Christmas Star" and "Music of the Spheres," for the university community as well as the general public. Approximately 2,500 K–12 students visited the UNK Planetarium in 2004–05. In addition, the department visits local schools to present science lectures and demonstrations. The observatory is open on regularly scheduled nights for public viewing.

Loren Killion

As one of only nine Loper basketball players to be named All-American, Loren Killion set a number of school records during his career, which lasted from 1974 to 1977. Among them, he set the career mark for most points scored (2,100), most field goals (903), and most field goal attempts (1,828) as well as the seasonal record for scoring (715 in 1977). Killion is also listed among the school's top basketball players in career rebounding (922), career steals (121), and seasonal rebounding (239 in 1975). He also played professional basketball in Belgium. Inducted into the UNK Athletic Hall of Fame in 1989, Killion is now president of the Loper Athletic Club.

❖ **OTHER PROGRAMS**

When Kearney joined the University of Nebraska system, the nursing program became the fourth division of the University of Nebraska Medical Center's College of Nursing. The Kearney division not only offers a baccalaureate nursing program that includes LPN-to-BSN and RN-to-BSN programs but through distance education technology, grants both master's and doctoral degrees in the central Nebraska area. More than 800 nurses have graduated, and half practice in the region.

One of the newer options on campus, the women's studies program, offers an interdisciplinary minor that complements UNK's liberal arts core courses. The program began in 1989, the result of an ad hoc committee formed by President Nester to consider women's issues on campus. First directed by English professor Kate Benzel, the program involves all aspects of the campus—academics, student services, and extracurricular groups. In 2001 the three women's studies directors from UNL, UNO, and UNK began a collaboration to strengthen their programs. As a result, they initiated a No Limits Conference that rotates annually among the campuses, and every other year the directors offer a Feminist Teaching Institute for faculty of all three campuses who are interested in teaching women's study courses.

For place-bound, nontraditional, working adults, the Division of Continuing Education has begun offering e-Campus, graduate and

◆ Richard Kopf

Federal Judge Richard Kopf graduated from KSC in 1969 and earned his law degree from the University of Nebraska College of Law in 1972. From 1972 to 1974 he worked as a law clerk for the Honorable Donald Ross, U.S. circuit judge. He then returned to his hometown of Lexington, Nebraska, to go into private practice from 1974 to 1986. In 1987 he was selected to serve as U.S. magistrate judge for the U.S. District Court for the district of Nebraska. In 1992 he was nominated by President George H.W. Bush to serve in his current position as chief U.S. district judge for the district of Nebraska.

undergraduate degree programs and endorsements, to off–campus students in various formats. Videoconference courses are delivered to sites throughout Nebraska by satellite, IP, or a fiber-optic network. For online courses, students need only a computer with Internet capability and may "attend" class any time of the day or week. Similar to traditional courses, students work interactively with an instructor. Face-to-face courses as well as blended courses are also available at a few sites in central Nebraska.

Continuing education also supports the Elderhostel program for adults 55 and older from across the United States and around the world. These one-week, all-inclusive courses include meals, lectures, field trips, and medical and insurance coverage. UNK annually presents six programs: two focusing on the sandhill cranes, two on birding, one on fossils, and another on the prairie pioneer.

COMPUTER ❖ TECHNOLOGY

Computer technology has brought about the most dramatic changes on campus, initiating a new age in higher education. On campus since the 1960s, computers were not used extensively until 1991 when Ludden, Mantor, and Centennial Towers provided computer labs for students. The library went online in 1991 with an automated card catalogue system that allowed students to search the library from any building at any time, to tie into the libraries at the other state colleges as well as the university system, and to access national and international networks. Librarians could also check out materials with scanning wands, and Interlibrary Loan enhanced their services. By 1995, thanks to a $1.58 million Kiewit grant, all faculty enjoyed networked computer stations in their offices and could access the Internet for the first time. The next year UNK posted its first home page, and Stout Hall became the first residence hall that wired all rooms for Internet access. Since 1999 Information Technology Services has established e-mail accounts for

Students and professor in the College of Education computer lab

every UNK student, wired every residence hall for internet access, and equipped every dorm with a computer lab for student use. Currently, wireless Internet access is expanding across the campus, and the UNK Web site is acquiring a new, unified look.

The ongoing installation of multimedia "smart" classrooms in academic buildings began with a grant from the University of Nebraska Foundation in 1994 and continues through student technology fees. These classrooms now offer faculty and students the latest in audiovisual educational aids, featuring computer terminals with CD/DVD capability, video players, overhead projectors, and large projection screens, to complement the learning experience. Another classroom tool, the Blackboard Learning System, enables faculty to interact with their students over the Internet or teach online courses.

The administration has also benefited from advanced technology. In 1992 UNK became one of the first schools in the United States to convert to the SIS Plus version of maintaining student records and developed the first voice-activated, telephone registration in Nebraska. Beginning in 1993, students could even register over the Internet. UNK has committed itself to becoming a national leader in employing information technology to enhance teaching and learning, especially at the undergraduate level.

Students using a computer lab in the library

The library has initiated dramatic Internet and database advances as well. In 2005, in addition to the 400,000 books, 225,000 government documents, 1,100,000 microforms, and 1,630 periodical subscriptions in its collection, it offers students the ability to access 97 computer databases, web-based indexes that provide access to the full text of 16,000 electronic journals and magazines, and the Internet. In addition, Interlibrary Loan provides students and faculty access to PDFs of journal articles from other libraries that they can download to or print from their personal computers.

100 NOTABLE PEOPLE

Douglas A. Kristensen

In July 2002 Douglas A. Kristensen, a native of Minden, Nebraska, and the former and longest-serving Speaker of the Nebraska Legislature, succeeded Gladys Styles Johnston as the university's chancellor. Kristensen earned a bachelor's degree in economics and political science at UNL in 1977 and a JD from Drake University in 1980. He took part in numerous campus activities and events long before his appointment. While a representative of the 37th legislative district, which includes Kearney, he was one of the sponsors of the bill proposing to include KSC in the University of Nebraska system.

STUDENT LIFE ❖

Students have long known that college offers more than academic opportunities and that social and extracurricular activities play a large role in their university experience. At one time the preceptress hovered over her charges, attempting to isolate them from the wicked influences of the outside world with strict regulations; mandatory daily chapel attendance reinforced this concept. However, shirttail parades, panty raids, and streaking proved to authorities that occasionally students "just want to have fun." Channeling this attitude into positive learning experiences for students has been one of the greatest challenges at Kearney over the past 100 years.

Lessening the restrictions and offering more choices in residence hall living proved to be successful. Although KSC experimented with coed residence halls as early as the 1980s, with men on one floor and women on another, they discovered that students desired more options. Designating the new University Residence North and University Residence South as housing for the Greek chapters was the first step for UNK in 1991. Although fraternities had long established their own off-campus housing, sororities had only inadequate communities on designated residence hall floors. A closer unity within each organization as well as with each other resulted.

Students in a residence hall lounge

Revisions in the other residence halls followed, and by 2004 students over 20 years of age could choose floors that featured independent living with cooking facilities. Coeducational living by floor or suite continues, but rather than isolating men and women on separate floors, the university assigns them to alternating rooms or suites on the same floor with separate bathroom facilities.

LEARNING ❖
COMMUNITIES

The latest concept that weaves social and academic interests is the new emphasis on learning communities. Students interested in a highly structured study environment may choose to live together in the Stout or Randall Honors Halls. Here students share an academic atmosphere and socialize with others of similar ambitions. A Future Teacher Learning Community began in the fall of 2001 that presently supports undergraduate education students who live on a designated residence hall floor and enroll in a common core of classes that prepares them for teaching. The Business Learning Community also connects students in a cohort group who take courses, work on projects, and participate in programs together to make them more successful students and business executives. Those who opt to devote one year of their academic careers to working on a problem facing a local community live together in the political science department's Community for Active Citizenship. Partnering with faculty members, students research a problem, create and enact a plan of action to address it, and then evaluate the results.

Student teaching in a grade school

Other communities focus on balancing students' personal lives. The UNK Service Learning Community provides opportunities for students to become engaged in civic affairs and work in volunteer organizations in Kearney or in their home communities. Students may tutor, work in youth centers, serve as mentors, provide companionship to persons with disabilities or the elderly, assist teachers with at-risk students, help at preschools, or coach. Another choice, the Healthy Lifestyle Learning Community, promotes positive personal growth and wellness in a group that supports personal choices.

❖ **INTERNATIONAL OPPORTUNITIES**

UNK continues to encourage students to expand their cultural boundaries. Originating in the early 1970s with the study abroad program sponsored by the Department of Foreign Languages, the first comprehensive Office of International Education began as KSC became part of the university system. Between 1991 and 1995, foreign student enrollment grew from 111 to 265, rising to nearly 5 percent of the entire student body by 2001. In 1989 President Nester combined study abroad, international student advising, international studies, and all international initiatives into one program to create the Office of International Education in Student Affairs. He appointed Jerry Fox as its part-time director. A 1995 reorganization streamlined the Office of International Education and created the Office of Multicultural and International Student Services. When this program outgrew its facility, the college created two separate offices, one serving multicultural students and another aiding international students. Currently, the Office of International Education directs the international studies program while assisting students with orientation, acculturation, and immigration matters and arranges study abroad opportunities for UNK students.

International education also organizes the James E. Smith Midwest Conference on World Affairs to involve students in global citizenship. In 1994 the conference leadership began rotating among four undergraduate

R. SIVARAMA KRISHNAN

R. Sivarama Krishnan was KSC's first international professor. He came to UNK after earning his BS, MA, and MS degrees at the University of Madras, India, and his PhD at Texas A&M University. He taught Chemistry from 1972 to 1994. He also served as mentor to Vani Kotcherlakota, professor of economics and the University's first international female professor. Kotcherlakota received a BA from Andhra University in India, dual MA degrees from the University of Western Ontario in Canada and Queen's University (also in Canada) and earned her PhD from Andhra University. She has taught at UNK since 1986 and has acted as department chair.

World Affairs Conference in the Student Union

◆ Tom Kropp

Tom Kropp returned to KSC as a graduate assistant in 1979 and became co–head basketball coach in 1991 and head coach in 1997. As a student he played football and basketball at the school and was selected in both the NFL and NBA drafts. He played several years in the NBA for the Chicago Bulls and the Washington Bullets and abroad. Kropp has since coached the basketball team to nine trips to the NCAA Division II Tournament, including its fourth consecutive appearance in 2005, and three trips to the North Central Regional Finals (Sweet Sixteen). Among numerous other honors, Kropp was named by *Sports Illustrated* as one of Nebraska's 50 greatest athletes of the 20th century and one of the state's 10 greatest sports celebrities. He was also inducted into the Nebraska State Athletic Hall of Fame.

colleges, each deciding on a theme that reflected its area of specialization. For example, in 1997 the College of Education chose "Children's Rights and Our Responsibilities" and in 2000 the College of Fine Arts and Humanities selected "Images of Culture." One highlight of the conference is the keynote speaker, an internationally known scholar, activist, or politician. In addition, the International Student Association, sponsored by Morris Press, annually showcases the native cuisine and folk art of the many foreign students who attend KSC.

In 1997 Director Fox established an exchange program with the University of Rostock, Germany, presenting opportunities for students from various departments. In 2001 and 2002, UNK construction management students worked on a joint construction project with Rostock construction engineering students to build the first wood structures in northern Germany, winning a $20,000 award for their project. In addition, UNK participants in the global sources information technology program studied e-commerce in Rostock, and education students experienced different teaching techniques in German schools.

Beginning in 2000 the Office of International Education arranged to Japanese students to campus as part of a national collegiate network program. Approximately 200 Japanese students enroll each year at UNK in a four-year program. During the 2004–5 year, 286 undergraduates, 27 postgraduates, 51 English Language Institute students, and 18 exchange program students from 50 different countries studied at UNK. In addition, the national student exchange program allows UNK students to attend another university or college for up to one academic year, often at UNK tuition rates. They may choose from 177 member campuses in the United States, the District of Columbia, three territories, and four Canadian provinces, and

Exchange students from Japan

the credits they earn are recorded on their UNK transcript. Kearney is the only institution of higher learning in Nebraska that offers this program.

Departments sponsor their own international programs as well. The social work department sponsors an International Social Work Experience every two years consisting of a 13- to 16-day tour to countries such as Israel, Sweden, Denmark, Norway, Finland, and China. Students visit foreign agencies and family gatherings, listen to lectures by educators and leaders, and experience volunteer and community work. Participants interact with locals, experience different customs, and expand their understanding of the global community. Study Abroad in Mexico, sponsored by the Department of Modern Languages for 27 years, has remained vibrant, and 11 groups have gone to Guadalajara since 1991. In coordination with the Universidad de Guadalajara, students live with Mexican families and attend an intensive five-week program with classes four hours a day, five days a week at the Foreign Student Study Center. After classes end, student can enroll in workshops such as Mexican pottery, Mexican folk dance, contemporary Latin dance, guitar and singing, and Mexican cuisine.

100 NOTABLE PEOPLE

Max McFarland ❖

Max McFarland, professor of counseling and school psychology, received his BS, MSEd, and EdS degrees from KSC in 1975, 1976, and 1977, and an EdD in school psychology from the University of South Dakota in 1986. In 2003 he became UNK's fourth faculty member to receive a University of Nebraska system-wide Outstanding Teaching and Instructional Creativity Award. In addition to coordinating National Association of School Psychologist accreditation for the School Psychology Program and establishing the Professional Development Seminar Series, McFarland has worked to strengthen the school psychology program at UNK and has won UNK Creative Teaching Awards in 2002 and 2003 as well as a Pratt-Heins award for teaching in 1999.

Mardi Gras in the Student Union

❖ **STUDENT ORGANIZATIONS**

A wide array of organizations combine social and academic interests in every UNK department. The most active in the College of Business and Technology include the Accounting Society, which annually assists individuals with their tax returns and has helped with Habitat for Humanity, Salvation Army food drives, and Red Cross blood drives. Another, the Financial Leaders Association, takes an annual trip to a metropolitan financial district, visiting New York City in 2005. The Students in Free Enterprise organization is currently investigating a project that may eventually lead to a new business at UNK—a high-tech laser used in

◆ **Rosella Meier**

When KSC decided to launch volleyball as a new sport in the late 1960s, it selected Rosella Meier, a 1965 graduate, as the program's first coach. Meier accepted the position in 1968 and by 1972 the team finished with a 15-1 record and its first state championship. Meier's teams won 11 district championships during the 20 years they were NAIA members, and they won 9 championships during the 14 years they were members of the Central States Conference. Meier's record at the time of her retirement was 650-225-9, the best of any coach in any sport at the institution.

industrial technology classes that could create anything from engraved trophies and plaques to glass paperweights and chess sets—and would give students hands-on experience at running a company.

Education honorary Chi Sigma Iota hosted its first annual Justice for All Conference in 2001, which addressed diversity and justice issues related to persons of color and sexual orientation, and sponsored an Agency Fair that provided an opportunity for students to network with local service agencies. Sigma Tau Delta, the English honorary, continues to showcase student creative writing. They publish the *Carillon* and sponsor poetry slams, contests between student and faculty poets reading their works. The UNK Art Society promotes the annual Student Juried Art Exhibition and sponsors the Artists of Kearney Studio Tour.

Students in natural and social sciences participate in wide-ranging activities. The Criminal Justice Club sponsors field trips to institutions such as the Nebraska Penitentiary, Lincoln Correctional Center, Leavenworth (Kansas) Federal Prison, the military prison at Fort Leavenworth, the Norton (Kansas) Prison, and the Nebraska Center for Women. In addition, students participate in ride-a-longs with various police departments and tour the state police headquarters, State Police Forensics Laboratory, Girls and Boys Town, and the Drug Rehabilitation Treatment Center. The club also conducted a mock crime scene investigation with the Kearney/Buffalo County Law Enforcement Center. In 2002 the UNK Geography Club sponsored Earth Daze, a three-day environmental celebration. The department also hosted the Geographic Educators of Nebraska Summer Workshop titled "Space Photography in Education," featuring educators from Texas as well as UNK faculty with NASA expertise. The national office of the history honor society, Phi Alpha Theta, has presented the "Best Chapter" award in Division III to UNK several times, and in 2004 the chapter co-hosted the regional conference in Omaha.

Students participating in an art workshop

Women's studies students have organized Iota Iota Iota, a national women's honorary society. They have also begun sponsoring V-Day activities, a global movement to raise awareness and stop violence against women and girls. Another group, the Student Hispanic Association, has hosted the Cultural Unity Conference for Hispanic high school students. Sessions focus on scholarships and grants, opportunities for minorities in the job market, and immigration, citizenship, and student life.

Student Health has recently instituted peer health education on campus to provide information to help students make healthy decisions regarding sex, alcohol, body image, and smoking prevention/cessation. Peer Educators, 13 select students, are all certified by Baccus and Gamma, a nationally recognized peer health education organization.

Faith groups also serve students. The Cooperative Campus Ministries, comprised of individual campus religious organizations, supports students struggling with spiritual and emotional concerns, such as the September 11, 2001, terrorist attacks and the war in Iraq, and offers social activities, such as hayrack rides and barn dances. When some of the groups identified pornography as a problem on campus, the group worked together to present a program to students concerning the issues. In addition, the Christian Student Fellowship regularly holds services, designed and run by UNK students, in the Nebraskan Student Union.

❖ **GREEK LIFE**

Sigma Lambda Beta members

Sororities and fraternities add another dimension to student life, and their shared quarters in the on-campus residence halls have enhanced the brother- and sisterhoods. In 2004 over 600 men and women, about 10 percent of the student population, belonged to the Greek community. The current sororities, Alpha Omicron Pi, Alpha Phi, Chi Omega, and Gamma Phi Beta, and

◆ Daniel Mowrey

Daniel Mowrey graduated summa cum laude from KSC in 1973 and earned a master's in mathematics (1975) and a PhD (1980) from Iowa State University. He then went to work for Eli Lilly, a pharmaceutical company in Indianapolis, Indiana, where he has been involved in the development of five new animal drug applications (NADAs), worked on two patents, and collaborated with colleagues on more than 50 papers as a senior research scientist. As a student at KSC, Mowrey was also a four-year letter winner in wrestling. He qualified for the national tournament three times. UNK awarded him a Distinguished Alumni Award in 1995.

the current fraternities, Alpha Tau Omega, Delta Tau Delta, Phi Delta Theta, Pi Kappa Alpha, Sigma Phi Epsilon, and Sigma Tau Gamma, are founded on the principles of friendship and the promotion of academic success. The Inter-fraternity Council for men and the Panhellenic Council for women unite all of the organizations to promote Greek life as well as scholarship, leadership, and service among its members.

Established at UNK in 1991 and nationally recognized in 1993, Delta Tau Delta is the newest social fraternity and in 2003 received the Hugh Shields Award, the highest honor among the 119 Delta chapters. Phi Kappa Tau, which disbanded in 1997, is currently recolonizing at UNK with the support of alumni. Recruitment began in the spring of 2005, and the group hopes for a new charter within the next two years. A Latino-based fraternity, Sigma Lambda Beta, has also begun to colonize.

Community service and philanthropic projects have long been a part of Greek organizations, but participation levels have increased in recent years. Chapters choose a local cause as well as a national or international philanthropy and donate their time to raise funds for worthy causes, such as Habitat for Humanity, and the I Believe in Me Ranch, National Kidney Foundation, Make-A-Wish Foundation, Salvation Army, and Heart Fund. In 2003 the Greeks raised more than $27,000 for local and national charities and volunteered nearly 13,000 hours for community service.

Student organizations and activities add fullness to student life at UNK. All promote academic excellence, support student creativity and research, encourage social interaction among students, provide emotional and spiritual support, and expand student horizons with new experiences beyond themselves and into the community—in Kearney and in the world.

ROCKY MOUNTAIN ❖ ATHLETIC CONFERENCE

In many respects, joining the NCAA Division II in 1989 posed hefty challenges for the Kearney athletic program. For three seasons, the college was forced to compete as an independent, adjusting to an increased level of competition while searching for a conference willing to expand. Unfortunately for the athletes who competed from 1990 to 1993, competing without a conference also meant foregoing the chance to win league championships and awards. In July 1994, however, UNK joined the Rocky Mountain Athletic Conference (RMAC). The school immediately created one of the most respectable programs in the conference.

With the formation of women's golf that same year, UNK claimed a total of 16 sports, 8 men's and 8 women's. The list of programs included football, basketball, wrestling, track, cross country, golf, tennis, and baseball for men, and volleyball, basketball, swimming and diving, track, cross country, golf, tennis, and softball for women.

Volleyball team playing in the Health and Sports Center

Three of UNK's strongest sports programs—volleyball, football, and basketball—continue to pile on victories. In 1992 Rosella Meier, the only volleyball coach in UNK history at the time, retired after 24 years of coaching. She departed as the winningest coach in school history, leaving behind a 650–225–9 record that was, at the time, ranked in the top 10 nationally on the all-time coaching list.

Even after Meier's retirement, the volleyball program continued its string of victories. The 1995 and 1996 teams, under the guidance of new head coach Patty Sitorius, reached the NCAA Division II Elite Eight Tournament, the equivalent of the NCAA Division I Final Four. In 1999 Rick Squiers took over the head-coaching position and led the team to its first ever RMAC title. His teams repeated their showing in the Elite Eight tournament by earning back-to-back trips in 2003 and 2004. The 2004 team was just the fourth team ever in NCAA II volleyball history to finish the regular season undefeated. Ranked first in the nation that year, the team lost to second-ranked (and also undefeated) Truman State of Missouri in the NCAA National tournament semifinals.

Rosella Meier

The football program also experienced the loss of a successful head coach. Claire Boroff retired in 1999 after 28 years at the helm of the program. He, too, left as one of the most successful coaches in UNK history, with a record of 169–105–5. Three years later, in 2002, the team, now led by Boroff's replacement Darrell Morris, finished 9–2, captured a share of the RMAC title, and made the 16-team NCAA II playoffs for the first time in school history. Morris experienced his first non-winning season in 2003 when, despite setting new school records for offensive yards in a season (5,062) and total average offensive yards per game (506.2), the Lopers ended the season 5–5 and 4–4 in conference play. The team finished with a losing record of 5–6 and 4–4 (RMAC) in 2004.

Claire Boroff

CHAMPIONSHIPS

1995:   RMAC Men's Golf,
         RMAC Softball,
         Women's Tennis,
         Volleyball

1996:   RMAC Men's Golf,
         RMAC Women's
         Basketball,
         Softball

1997:   RMAC Men's Golf,
         RMAC Women's
         Basketball,
         Softball

1998:   RMAC Men's Basketball,
         Men's Golf,
         Men's Indoor Track,
         RMAC Softball

1999:   RMAC Men's Golf,
         Men's Indoor Track,
         RMAC Women's
         Basketball,
         Women's Golf,
         Softball,
         Volleyball

2000:   RMAC Men's Indoor
         Track,
         Wrestling,
         RMAC Women's
         Basketball

2001:   RMAC Men's Indoor
         Track,
         RMAC Women's
         Basketball

2002:   RMAC Men's Indoor
         Track,
         Wrestling,
         RMAC Women's Track

2003:   RMAC Men's Basketball,
         Football,
         Men's Indoor Track,
         Wrestling,
         RMAC Women's
         Basketball,
         Softball,
         Women's Track

2004:   RMAC Men's Tennis,
         Wrestling,
         RMAC Women's
         Basketball

2005:   RMAC Men's Basketball,
         Men's Tennis,
         Wrestling,
         RMAC Volleyball

Football

Men's basketball

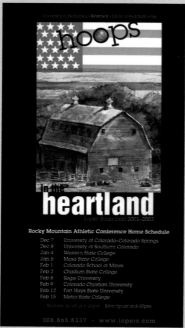

Men's and women's basketball poster

Women's basketball

Indoor track

Softball

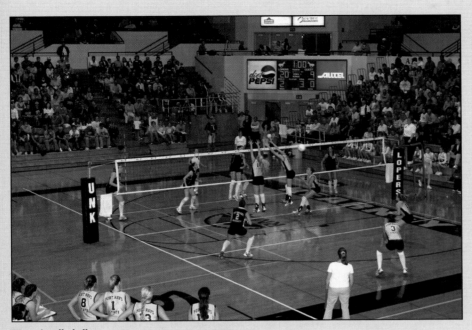

Women's volleyball

Women's basketball

Wrestling

Women's swimming

Baseball

Fans at a Loper football game

Earl Rademacher

Earl Rademacher, a 1954 KSTC graduate and tennis letterman, has served UNK in a myriad of ways as an administrator and a faculty member since his career began at the university in 1960. Initially hired as assistant to the registrar and director of admissions, he was promoted to the institution's chief financial officer in 1975. He served as acting president from August 1, 1982, until March 1, 1983, after the resignation of President Brendan McDonald. Rademacher retired in 1996 as UNK's vice chancellor of business and finance, and in 2004 a plaza on the west side of the Alvie and Ruth Payne Family Bridge was dedicated in his honor.

Basketball has been another steady draw at the university. In 2001 the women's team, led by seven-year head coach Amy Stephens, set a new NCAA II record for consecutive home victories. In February the team defeated Fort Hays State University (Kansas) 97–78 for their 86th consecutive home win. The record ended at 87 wins a year later, but the women pulled off at least a 10-game winning streak every year in each of the eight seasons leading up to the 2002–3 season.

Even though Stephens left the program in 2002 to accept an assistant coaching position at her alma mater, the University of Nebraska–Lincoln, her replacement, Carol Russell, guided the team to its sixth consecutive RMAC championship and its eighth overall in 2004. The 2004 team also earned a trip to the NCAA Division II Tournament for the ninth straight year. But the

Captains of the football team

Men's basketball team playing in the Health and Sports Center

work ethic did not end on the court. During the 2002–3 academic year, the Loper women recorded the highest grade point average (3.723) for all women's basketball programs in the nation, including the NCAA, the NAIA, and junior college programs.

The men's basketball team reached its first Elite Eight tournament during the 2002–3 season. With school bests of a 30–3 record and a 23-game winning streak, the Loper men cracked the number two spot in the national polls that year and topped all NCAA II schools in attendance, averaging 3,839 fans at each game. As many as 6,016 fans, the largest crowd in UNK history, arrived at the coliseum to watch the team play Fort Hays State. The men's team won RMAC championships in 1998 and 2003.

❖ **OTHER SPORTS**

While the so-called core sports have seemed to flourish at UNK, others have not been so lucky. An exception is wrestling. Before the arrival of current head coach Marc Bauer in 1999, the team cracked the top 10 at the NCAA II National Wrestling Championship four times; they finished 10th in 1992 and 1993 under head coach Ed Scantling, and 7th and 9th in 1995 and 1998, respectively, under head coach Jeff Cardwell. In 2003, Bauer led the team to its best showing ever: a runner-up finish in the national tournament.

Four wrestlers have been crowned NCAA II national champions: Jeff Sylvester (197 lbs) in 2004, Frank Kuchera (174 lbs) in 2003 Brian Hagan (118) in 1990, and Ali Amiri (150 lbs) in and 1991 and 1990. The team's grade point average of 3.519 in 2004 was the highest of all NCAA II wrestling programs and the best GPA ever recorded in the 11-year history of the award, presented by the Wrestling Coaches Association.

Although the softball program won four straight RMAC championships from 1995 to 1998 and finished runner-up at the NCAA II national championships in 1999, most other sports' major accomplishments have come at the individual level. As a team, the men's cross country program has placed in several NCAA national meets, including top 10 finishes in 1990 (8th), 1991

1999 softball team

Jean Sullivan Rawson

In 2004 Jean Sullivan Rawson, a 1940 graduate of KSTC, left to the University of Nebraska Foundation a $7 million gift from her estate. Of that $7 million, $3.5 million was used to create a permanent endowment at UNK. The Jean Sullivan Rawson and Richard Rawson Scholarship will provide annual scholarships to graduates of Nebraska high schools who demonstrate financial need. The other $3.5 million was set aside for an endowed student scholarship at the University of Nebraska Technical College of Agriculture in Curtis, from which Mrs. Rawson graduated in 1936 when the college was an agriculture high school. Rawson earned her business degree from KSTC in 1940 and played oboe and English horn in the school's student music groups. She also edited the student newspaper.

◆ **Robert Rycek**

Robert Rycek, professor of psychology and associate dean of the College of Natural and Social Sciences, is UNK's third recipient of the University of Nebraska system-wide Outstanding Teaching and Instructional Creativity Award, which he received in 2001. Rycek graduated from the University of Illinois, Chicago and earned his MA and PhD at Northern Illinois University. He has also received a Pratt-Heins Award for Service (2004) and back-to-back UNK Creative Teaching Awards (2000, 2001).

(2nd), 1992 (3rd), 1994 (4th), and 1995 (7th). The 1994 NCAA meet was held at UNK. Luke Garringer qualified for the meet in 2004. On the women's side, the Lopers regularly compete against Adams State (Colorado) and Western State (Colorado), which have both won national NCAA championships.

When the new Health and Sports Center was completed in 1991, the basketball court walls in Cushing Coliseum were removed to create a 176-yard, 8-lane indoor track. Since then, the men's and women's indoor track teams have had numerous All-Americans. From 1998 to 2003, the men won six straight RMAC indoor titles, while the Loper women won back–to–back RMAC titles in 2002 and 2003. Janet Boetcher won two national titles for the school, first in the indoor 20-pound weight throw in 1999 and again in the hammer throw in 2000. The women's track and field team won its first RMAC outdoor track and field championship in 2002 and followed up with a defense of its title in 2003.

The baseball program enjoyed only three winning seasons during the 1990s, as they did during the past two decades, but several players earned individual honors. Since 1993 seven Lopers earned all-region honors at the NCAA Division II level, and several were named to an all-conference baseball team. In 2002 head coach Guy Murray retired after 29 seasons, and UNK hired Damon Day, a head coach at Dana College for four years and a Great Plains Athletic Conference Coach of the Year award winner, to lead the program into a new era.

Although the women's tennis team has yet to win a conference championship, the UNK men captured their first RMAC tennis championship in 2004 under head coach Patrick Fischer by beating number one seed Colorado School of Mines 5–0. When Fischer left the program to pursue an athletic

Hurdlers running on the indoor track in Cushing Coliseum

Men's golf

DiAnna Schimek

Nebraska State Senator DiAnna Schimek graduated from KSC with a BA in 1963. She taught history, political science, and business in Colorado and Nebraska and was a member of the Democratic National Committee from 1976 to 1988 before being elected to the state legislature in 1988. Schimek was re-elected to her position as senator from the 27th District in 1992, 1996, 2000, and 2004. She is currently the longest-serving woman in the legislature and is a member of the following committees: Government, Military and Veterans' Affairs (chairperson); Business and Labor; Urban Affairs; and the Committee on Committees.

administration career in Europe, Jesse Plote, an assistant men's coach at Creighton University, became both the men's and women's tennis coach

The golf program, despite experiencing limited team success, has qualified for the Northwest/West Super Regional Tournament every year since 2001, when the NCAA switched to a new format to determine which teams and individuals would make the NCAA II championships. Two women golfers have qualified for the NCAA Division II Women's Golf Tournament. Carla Dobchuck participated in the meet three times. She finished 24th in 1999, 4th in 2000, and 3rd in 2001, while Jenny Deines qualified for the meet in 2001 and 2002 and finished 24th and 5th, respectively. C. J. Farber is the only UNK linkster to receive All-American honors (1999).

Swimmers have also achieved individual success. A year before joining the NCAA II, Stefanie Seamon placed 4th for UNK in the 100-meter backstroke and 6th in the 50-meter freestyle at the NAIA championships. A year later in 1991, Yohara Salinas qualified for the NCAA II meet and placed in the 100-meter breaststroke, the 200-meter breaststroke, and in the 200-meter individual medley. No other swimmer or diver reached the national meet until diver Dusty Walston qualified for the NCAA Division II Swimming and Diving Championships in 2000. Although unable to participate in the meet due to a knee injury, Walston qualified for the meet again in 2001 and 2002, placing 8th in the one-meter board in 2002 and becoming only the second UNK swimmer or diver to receive All-American honors since 1991. When Walston graduated in 2002, she owned every possible UNK record in the one-meter and three-meter events. In 2005 diver Jennifer Atterbury also qualified for national competition.

❖ **Kenya Taylor**

In February 2005 the University of Nebraska awarded Kenya Taylor, professor and chair of the Department of Communication Disorders, an Outstanding Teaching and Instructional Creativity Award (OTICA), making her the fifth person at UNK to win the award since 1992. An authority in audiology and speech/language pathology, Taylor researches hearing loss and audiologic rehabilitation programs. Her students have achieved a first-time pass rate for accreditation of 92 percent compared to the national first-time pass rate of 79.8 percent.

CONFERENCE ❖ TITLES

During the 2003–4 season, UNK seized RMAC conference titles in men's tennis, women's basketball, and wrestling. The university placed second in volleyball, men's basketball, men's indoor track and field, women's indoor track and field, and women's outdoor track and field. Each of those sports qualified for NCAA II national championships and was enough to earn the school its ninth consecutive all-sports trophy. Awarded each year to the institution that accumulates the most points based on its teams' final performance in the four core sports of football (or men's soccer), volleyball, and men's and women's basketball, and four wild card sports (determined by the school's two best finishes in 13 potential Olympic sports), the RMAC Wells Fargo Cup is evidence of UNK's overall success in athletics. As the school undergoes yet another upgrade to Foster Field with the installation of synthetic field turf and other improvements that include refurbishing the west grandstands and installing new east bleachers, lighting and sound equipment, a locker room building near the north end zone, and a new scoreboard, school athletics appears poised for another era of expansion and success.

Foster Field renovations and future site of Ron and Carol Cope Stadium

CONCLUSION ❖

Remarkable changes have occurred over the past 100 years. When classes opened in 1905, the campus consisted of 20 acres, a former apartment house for a dormitory, an Administration building that housed all classrooms and offices, and a faculty of 21, including the principal, preceptress, and librarian, to educate Nebraska students. Today the university spreads across nearly 260 acres with 37 buildings, 245 full-time tenure and tenure-track faculty, 54 full-time other faculty, and 93 part-time faculty to educate students from around the world. In 1905 students paid a one-time matriculation fee of $5, tuition and books were free, and room and board cost approximately $15–$30; in 2004–5 tuition and fees for residents averaged $4,260, room and board, $4,952, and books about $754. The first student body totaled 400. Today more than 6,540 students from all 93 Nebraska counties, 36 states, and 52 countries attend UNK.

However, the university's dedication to academic excellence has not wavered. In the words of A. O. Thomas, the school's first president, Kearney "is bound to be a great school. It cannot escape it." When Kearney State College celebrated becoming the University of Nebraska at Kearney on July 1, 1991, Senator and soon-to-be Chancellor Douglas Kristensen stated, "The honor and responsibility is from today forward. We've known Kearney to be the shining star, now it's the brightest light. I think this is the most aggressive, progressive campus in the university system, and it will continue to be that way." UNK is dedicated to taking Thomas's prophecy into the future.

Campus life

Future UNK students

Don Welch

Don Welch graduated from KSC in 1954 and began teaching a 15- to 18-hour course load in English and philosophy in 1958. He was appointed the school's first Reynolds Professor in Poetry and has won numerous awards for both teaching and poetry, including a Pratt-Heins Award for Teaching (1988), a Nebraska Board of Trustees Teaching Excellence Award (1990), the Pablo Neruda Prize for Poetry (1980), and the Nebraska Humanities Council Sower Award (2004). Welch was awarded a Distinguished Alumni Award from KSC in 1983 and retired in 1997. In 2001 a life-size statue of the renowned poet and educator was dedicated just south of the Calvin T. Ryan library.

ACKNOWLEDGEMENTS

Professor of English Susanne George Bloomfield, who earned her BA and MA from UNK and her PhD from UNL, holds the Martin Distinguished Professorship. She has received the Leland Holdt/Security Mutual Distinguished Faculty Award for Superior Teaching, Research, and Service, the Pratt-Heins Award for Excellence in Teaching, and the Mari Sandoz Award from the Nebraska Library Association for her literary contributions to the state. Among her publications are three biographies published by the University of Nebraska Press. In addition to *From the Beginning*, Bloomfield has also published *The Platte River*, *A Prairie Mosaic*, and *A Presidential Visit* for UNK

Professor of Art Richard Schuessler earned his BFA in Graphic Design from the State University of New York at Fredonia and a MFA in Visual Communications from Virginia Commonwealth University. Schuessler has been involved with the UNK Centennial Celebration since 2003. He and his students have also been responsible for the design and visual development of UNK's Centennial logo, banners, and historical posters. Schuessler has received a variety of design awards for art direction and design from Nebraska's American Institute of Graphic Arts and Advertising Federation organizations. He has been published in two graphic design textbooks and recognized for his Art Direction with design projects that have been nationally juried and published in *Print*, *Step by Step*, *How* and *CMYK* magazines. One of thirty-three "Profiles of Excellence" for outstanding faculty, *From the Beginning* will be his third UNK book design since 1999.

A graduate student of English, Eric Melvin Reed earned a BA from UNK in 2002 and an MA in History in 2003. He served as Managing Editor of the university's literary journal, *The Carillon*, in 2002 and has published articles in *The Carillon*, the *UNK Undergraduate Research Journal*, and for several computer magazines as a writer for Sandhills Publishing. He received an Honorable Mention award for his history thesis in 2003, and his essay "Structure, Metafiction, and the Real in Charlie Kaufman's *Adaptation*" won the critical essay award at the 2005 Sigma Tau Delta International Convention in Kansas City, Missouri.

Editorial Board:

Donald Briggs, Jack Karracker, Douglas Kristensen, John Lillis, Beverly Mathiesen, Kenneth Nikels, Earl Rademacher, Keith Terry, Ann Tillery, and Gary Zaruba

Design:

Richard Schuessler	Creative Director
Kriste Sumpter	Senior Director
Mark Hartman	Art Director (editor)
John Deitering	Art Director/Designer
Steve Valish	Art Director/Designer
Jamie Gall	Designer
Justin Leatherman	Designer
Eric Nyffeler	Designer
Elissa Sims	Designer

Production Artist:

Jeremy Bengtson, Chris Coffelt, Linda Price, Andrea Spencer

The design of *From the Beginning* was created and completed by students, staff, and faculty in the Art department. DPI GRAPHICS is a design course that emphasizes the creation of quality artwork and design for clients while providing students with invaluable design experience and professional artwork for their portfolios.

Photography Credits:

Baer Photography

Kearney Hub

The Nature Conservancy

UNK Alumni Association

UNK Archives

UNK Athletics

UNK Publications

Notable Credits:

A special thanks to Melissa A. Hudnall and to the students in Kate Benzel's English 101H composition course for their work on the *Centennial Celebration* posters and Charles Peek's English 101 students for their help in researching the college's *Antelope* student newspapers and the *Blue and Gold* annuals. John Lillis, UNK Archivist who assisted in archival research and prepared the index, as well as Jim Rundstrom, Director of Alumni Services, and Don Briggs, former Public Relations Director and Sports Information Director, deserve special recognition. Christine Gerber was in charge of promotion and marketing.

References for *From the Beginning* include the archives of the Calvin T. Ryan Library; Philip S. Holmgren's *Kearney State College 1905-1980: A History of the First Seventy-Five Years* and *Kearney 125: 1873-1998*; various issues of *Buffalo Tales* published by the Buffalo County Historical Society; *Where the Antelopes Play: A Brief Resumé of 20th Century Kearney Athletics* compiled by Douglas Banks and Donald Briggs; the *Antelope* (1910-2005); the *Blue and Gold* (1908-1990); and the *Kearney Hub* (1904-2005).

INDEX

D

E

F

G

M

N

O

P

Plambeck, Vernon, 100
planetarium, 143
Platte Valley Review, 100
Plote, Jesse, 159
Porter, George N., 7, 17, 18, 20, 25
Powell, Mr. and Mrs. R. W., 20
Pratt-Heins Foundation Awards, 122, 132
psychology program, 20

Quillen, Merlin, 70

Rademacher, Earl, 156
Rader, Kevin, 104
radio, 57
Raimondi, John, 117
Randall, Everett L., 21
Randall Hall, 46, 47
Rasmussen, Randy, 105
Raun, Robert, 121
Rawson, Jean Sullivan, 157
Raymond, Florence Hostetler, 14
Reasoner, Selma, 17
Recreation Club, 19
Reynolds, Wallace, 24
Reynolds Chair, 137
Reynolds Writers and Readers Series, 137
Richard Young Hospital, 81
Richmond, H. C., 8
Rifle and Pistol Club, 108
Robbins, Edith L., 4, 17
Roberts, Phyllis, 107, 127
Robinson, Alice M., 22
Rocky Mountain Athletic Conference, 152
Rodeo Club, 108, 109
Roland B. Welch Hall, 88, 91, 116
Ron and Carol Cope Cornerstone of Excellence Award, 129
Ron and Carol Cope Memorial Fountain, 122, 126, 127, 129
Rose, Gladys, 40
Rundstrom, Jim, 94
Rural Club, 19
Russell, Carol, 156
Ryan, Calvin T., 40, 48, 57, 63
Rycek, Robert, 140, 158

Salinas, Yohara, 159
Saunders, Mr. and Mrs. John, 12
Sawyer, Larry, 94
Scantling, Ed, 157
Schimek, DiAnna, 159
School of Business and Technology, 96
School of Education, 98
School of Fine Arts and Humanities, 99
School of Natural and Social Sciences, 102
Schuman, Earl, 98
Science Club, 63
Scott, Clayton, 71
Scott, Fran, 108
Seamon, Stefanie, 159
Senior Class play, 56
Senior Pedagogical Thesis, 17
Service Learning Community, 147
SEXPO, 105, 106
Shakespeare, bust of, 13
Sheldon, George L., 10
Shellberger Wing, 13
Shirt Tail Parade, 60
Sigma Lambda Beta, 151, 152
Sigma Phi Epsilon, 64, 110, 152

Sigma Tau Delta, 63, 100
Sigma Tau Gamma, 64, 152
Sigma Theta Phi, 23, 64
Sigma Upsilon Nu, 64
Simonson, Rick, 140
Single Tax, 24
Sipple, Leslie B., 19
Sitorius, Patty, 153
Skov, Leonard, 95
Smith, James E., 79, 93, 109
Smith, Lee R., 86
Smith, Marion C., 7, 13, 17, 23, 90
Smithey, Edith M., 64
Smithey, Wayne, 111
Snodgrass, M. R., 11, 21
Sodalistas Latina, 23
softball, 113, 115, 152, 154, 157
sororities, 109, 151
Spillway Park, 128
Sport Parachute Club, 108
Spruce, Georgeann, 101
SPURS, 110
Squiers, Rick, 153
St Cecilians, 18, 54
Staff Senate, 122
State College Education Association, 80
Steadman, Grace, 18, 23
Stenwall, Jill, 115
Stephens, Amy, 156
Stout, H. G., 40, 65
Stout Hall, 46, 47
Strawn, Robertson, 39
Stromquist, Eleanor, 59
Stryker, John, 24
Student Activities Council, 108
Student Alumni Foundation, 131
Student Army Training Corps, 13, 24
Student Council, 63, 106
Student Handbook, 106
Student Health and Counseling Center, 130
Student Health Services, 59, 106, 130, 151
Student Hispanic Association, 151
Student National Education Association, 63
Student Senate, 105
Student Support Services, 129
Student Union, 44, 45
Students in Free Enterprise, 149
Students' Bill of Rights, 105
Study Abroad in Mexico, 149
Stuff, Lillian, 59
Stumpff, Donald, 102
Stutheit, Bernhard F., 66
summer school, 51
Sunday School Lesson of the Air, 57
Sutton, H. O., 29
Sutton, Harriet, 48
Swan, H. W., 54, 94
Sweater Day, 60, 61
swimming, 72, 114, 152, 155, 159
Sylvester, Jeff, 157
Symphonic Wind Ensemble, 100

Tau Rho, 110
Taylor, Kenya, 160
Tegner Society, 23
tennis, 27, 68, 71, 72, 113, 158
Tennis Club, 30
The Courtin' Club, 30
The Hatchery, 44
The Merry Wives of Windsor, 18
The Oath of Knighthood, 13
The Spirit of Education, 48
Theater Arts League, 18, 43
Theta Chi, 110

❖ Donald Briggs has capably served the
University of Nebraska at Kearney since
the 1950s, promoting the campus while
preserving its history for generations to
come through his contributions to the
library archives. All who collaborated
on *From the Beginning*, as well as the
university community and its alumni,
owe him a huge debt of gratitude for
graciously sharing his inestimable
knowledge as well as his stockpile of
artifacts. Without his help, this book
would have taken longer to bring to
fruition and would bear far more inaccu-
racies than whatever errata might still
remain. Although he shrinks from publicity and acclaim, he should be singled
out for his extraordinary assistance.
Thank you, Don!